Misery Beyond Death

"This is that day when they will be unable to speak and they will not be permitted to offer any excuses. May misery be the end of the rejectors on that day." (77: 35-36)

By
Shaykh Mufti Saiful Islām

JKN Publications

© Copyright by JKN Publications

First Published in October 2020

ISBN 978-1-909114-64-7

British Library Cataloguing in Publication Data
A catalogue record for this book is available from the British Library.

All Rights Reserved. No part of this book may be reproduced, stored in a retrieval system or transmitted in any form or by any means, electronic, mechanical, photocopying, recording or otherwise, without the prior permission of the copyright owner.

Publisher's Note:

Every care and attention has been put into the production of this book. If however, you find any errors they are our own, for which we seek Allāh's ﷻ forgiveness and the reader's pardon.

Published by:

JKN Publications
118 Manningham Lane
Bradford
West Yorkshire
BD8 7JF
United Kingdom

t: +44 (0) 1274 308 456 | w: www.jkn.org.uk | e: info@jkn.org.uk

Book Title: Misery Beyond Death

Author: Shaykh Mufti Saiful Islām

Printed by Mega Printing in Turkey

*"In the Name of Allāh, the Most Beneficent,
the Most Merciful"*

Contents

Introduction...	5
Sūrah Mursalāt...	7
The Link with the Previous Sūrah...	9
Place of Revelation of Sūrah Mursalāt...	11
Oaths in the First Five Verses of Sūrah Mursalāt...	11
• First Meaning...	12
• Second Meaning...	14
• Third Meaning...	17
• Fourth Meaning...	18
Signs that will Commence the Day of Judgement...	23
Creation of Man...	43
The Punishment of Disbelief...	48
Quwwat-e-Nazriyyah...	49
Quwwat-e-Shahwiyyah...	50
Quwwat-e-Ghadhabiyyah...	50
The Earth as Our Home...	52
The Concept of Justice as Proof of God's Existence...	54
Reward of the Righteous...	70
Taqwa...	70
Food of Jannah...	72
Challenge to Mankind...	74
Translation of Sūrah Mursalāt...	77
Sūrah Mursalāt - Verses 1-10...	78
Sūrah Mursalāt - Verses 11-20...	79
Sūrah Mursalāt - Verses 21-29...	80
Sūrah Mursalāt - Verses 30-38...	81
Sūrah Mursalāt - Verses 39-47...	82
Sūrah Mursalāt - Verses 48-50...	83

Introduction

All praises are due to Allāh ﷻ. May peace, salutations and blessings be upon our guide and mentor, the final and beloved Prophet Muhammad ﷺ, upon his noble Sahābah ؓ, Tābi'īn and those who follow in their footsteps till the Day of Judgement. Āmīn.

One of the aspects which differentiates a Muslim from a non-Muslim is the belief in the Ākhirah (Hereafter). Muslims believe that they will be held accountable for wrongdoings and rewarded for good. This is the core aspect of the message in the holy Qur'ān to which Allāh ﷻ draws our attention throughout so that we believe in Him. In reinforcing this message, Allāh ﷻ describes extensively the scenes of the Day of Judgement.

Sūrah Mursalāt discusses in detail the catastrophic scenes on the Day of Judgement, when the record of deeds of each and every individual will be laid open in front of them. The shock and horror of that day will be extraordinary.

Although the holy Qur'ān discusses Jannah and Jahannam as an important element of the Hereafter, the main scenes will start as soon as the Day of Judgement takes place, from the blowing of the trumpet the first-time round to the reckoning of deeds starting. Sūrah Mursalāt focuses on these initial scenes. The detail throughout the sūrah indicates that although we view Jannah and Jahannam as the ultimate destinations, the initial scenes themselves on that day will become either a punishment or reward. These scenes will be precursors to what the ultimate ending of the individual is going to

Introduction

be, i.e. either Paradise or Hell.

My respected Shaykh, Muftī Saiful Islām Sāhib has completed this commentary of Sūrah Mursalāt which I have had the honour of assisting in compiling into a book format. One specific feature which I have noticed when Muftī Sāhib conducts tāfsīr, (and I have seen this being pointed out by other scholars as well) is that he will often mention all the related verses when doing commentary of one verse. Furthermore, astonishingly this is always done from his memory! He will use many verses to explain the subject of the original verse.

Scholars of tafsīr mention an important principle in relation to commentating on the holy Qur'ān:

اَلْقُرْاٰنُ يُفَسِّرُ بَعْضُهٗ بَعْضًا

"Parts of the Qur'ān elaborate on other parts of the Qur'ān."

This feature also alludes to the comprehensiveness of the holy Qur'ān.

May Allāh ﷻ allow us to do our accounts before our accounts will be done on the Day of Judgement and change our lives in accordance with the teachings of Islām. May Allāh ﷻ reward those who have assisted in the compilation of this book abundantly, especially my beloved teacher, Shaykh Mufti Saiful Islām Sāhib! Āmīn.

Zakiya Saeeda (Bukhārī Class)
August 2020/ Dhul-Hijjah 1441

Sūrah Mursalāt

All praises are due to our Creator and Sustainer; Allāh ﷻ, Lord of the worlds. May peace and blessings be upon our beloved leader and guide, Muhammad ﷺ, his noble Companions ؓ and his followers till the Last Day. Āmīn.

This sūrah commences by recounting the effects of revelation through the use of allegory; composed in the first five verses which incorporates a wide scope of meaning represented in each of the verses which Allāh ﷻ takes oath by. The forces of nature are referred to here; namely the wind. It not only benefits mankind in bringing together the blessings of rain and fertility, but also can blow turbulent gusts causing violent and uprooting forces to wreak havoc and destruction in our lives.

This is further depicted in a metaphorical sense. Hence, the winds can also be taken to represent the angels, the prophets or the holy Qur'ān. Many of the commentators have taken these meanings to be incorporated into the verses in which Allāh ﷻ takes oath.

The forces of nature which represent the air and wind is the medium through which divine revelation was carried as it descended down to the holy Prophet ﷺ. The same force of wind which is responsible in making nature submissive in benefiting us is also the same force which can cause nature to turn against us, in unleashing its destruction in the form of violent storms and hurricanes.

Just as the winds play a crucial role in promoting our well-being in the physical realm of our existence through the five oaths Allāh ﷻ takes in attributing qualities to the wind; the wind can also be used as an allegory to represent the prophets, angels or the holy Qur'ān in these five verses whose role is fostered in the spiritual realm of our existence.

Both the physical and spiritual realm of our lives need to co-exist side by side if mankind is to reap the benefits of this life and the next. Allāh ﷻ, in taking oath in the winds which is allegorical and can also refer to the spiritual realm of the messengers, angels and the holy Qur'ān, stresses these points further by taking oath. When Allāh ﷻ takes oath, this brings these points to our attention.

Those who fail to turn to Allāh ﷻ in repentance are warned against the punishment of the Hereafter, commencing with the destruction of every living thing, including the physical realm that we exist in. The sun, moon, planets and stars will all be destroyed before the Day of Judgement commences with the blowing of the trumpet the first time round.

Immediately, upon the trumpet being blown for the second time, all the people that ever existed on the face of this earth will be resurrected and brought together on the outstretched plain of this world. Then the reckoning of their deeds will begin.

The Link with the Previous Sūrah

The righteous will be recompensed with achieving success and salvation and the wrongdoers will be made to face the doom of untold misery in being punished in the Hellfire.

The Link with the Previous Sūrah

In Sūrah Insān, Allāh ﷻ mentions about the creation of mankind:

$$\text{إِنَّا خَلَقْنَا الْإِنسَانَ مِن نُّطْفَةٍ أَمْشَاجٍ نَّبْتَلِيهِ فَجَعَلْنَاهُ سَمِيعًا بَصِيرًا}$$

"Indeed, We have created man from a mixed seed to test him and We made him hearing and seeing." (76:2)

Allāh ﷻ says that He created mankind from a mixture of semen and He mentions about the purpose of creation. In sūrah Insān, Allāh ﷻ speaks about the beginning of creation, whereas in this sūrah, Allāh ﷻ is informing us about the ending of man. This worldly life is a test as Allāh ﷻ says:

$$\text{الَّذِي خَلَقَ الْمَوْتَ وَالْحَيَاةَ لِيَبْلُوَكُمْ أَيُّكُمْ أَحْسَنُ عَمَلًا ۚ وَهُوَ الْعَزِيزُ الْغَفُورُ}$$

"He has created death and life to test which of you carry out the best acts. He is the Mighty, the Most Forgiving." (67:2)

Allāh ﷻ bestowed us with the intellect to differentiate between right and wrong:

The Link with the Previous Sūrah

$$﴿إِنَّا هَدَيْنَاهُ السَّبِيلَ إِمَّا شَاكِرًا وَإِمَّا كَفُورًا﴾$$

"We guided him to the path (of the true religion) so he is either grateful (by following the path) or ungrateful (by choosing to remain a disbeliever)." (76:3)

In the previous sūrah, the mentioning of the delights of Jannah predominates and is mentioned extensively throughout the sūrah, although we are also reminded of the Hellfire at a glimpse. As with every sūrah, whenever there is mention of Jannah; Allāh ﷻ also mentions the punishment of Jahannam. The literal device of antithesis (mentioning the direct opposite) is used when Allāh ﷻ mentions His mercy alongside mentioning His punishment:

$$نَبِّئْ عِبَادِي أَنِّي أَنَا الْغَفُورُ الرَّحِيمُ ﴿٤٩﴾ وَأَنَّ عَذَابِي هُوَ الْعَذَابُ الْأَلِيمُ ﴿٥٠﴾$$

"Inform my bondsmen that I am certainly the Most Forgiving, the Most Merciful and that My punishment is definitely a most painful punishment." (15: 49-50)

Conversely, in Sūrah Mursalāt, the sūrah is predominated by the description of Jahannam, whereas only a brief mention is made of Jannah.

Place of Revelation of Sūrah Mursalāt

Sūrah Mursalāt was revealed in Makkah. Sayyidunā Abdullāh ibn Mas'ud ﷺ said:

بَيْنَمَا نَحْنُ مَعَ النَّبِيِّ فِي غَارٍ بِمِنًى إِذْ نَزَلَ عَلَيْهِ (وَالْمُرْسَلٰتِ) وَإِنَّهٗ لَيَتْلُوْهَا وَإِنِّيْ لَأَتَلَقَّاهَا مِنْ فِيْهِ وَإِنَّ فَاهُ لَرَطْبٌ بِهَا إِذْ وَثَبَتْ عَلَيْنَا حَيَّةٌ فَقَالَ النَّبِيُّ اقْتُلُوْهَا فَابْتَدَرْنَاهَا فَذَهَبَتْ فَقَالَ النَّبِيُّ وُقِيَتْ شَرَّكُمْ كَمَا وُقِيْتُمْ شَرَّهَا

"While we were with the Messenger of Allāh ﷺ in a cave at Minā, sūrah Mursalāt was revealed to him. He was reciting it and I was learning it from his mouth. Verily, his mouth was moist with it when a snake leaped out at us. The holy Prophet ﷺ said, 'Kill it!' So, we quickly went after it, but it got away. The holy Prophet ﷺ then said, 'It was saved from your harm just as you all were saved from its harm.'" (Bukhārī)

Oaths in the First Five Verses of Sūrah Mursalāt

وَالْمُرْسَلٰتِ عُرْفًا ۞١۞ فَالْعٰصِفٰتِ عَصْفًا ۞٢۞ وَالنّٰشِرٰتِ نَشْرًا ۞٣۞ فَالْفٰرِقٰتِ فَرْقًا ۞٤۞ فَالْمُلْقِيٰتِ ذِكْرًا ۞٥۞

"By the oath of those winds that are released to give benefit. By the oath of those winds that blow extremely severely. By the oath of those winds that spread out the clouds. By the oath of those winds that separate the clouds. By the oath of those winds that induce remembrance (of Allāh)." (77: 1-5)

The scholars have given four different interpretations for the first five verses of Sūrah Mursalāt:
1) Allāh ﷻ takes oath swearing by the winds.
2) Allāh ﷻ takes oath swearing by the angels.
3) Allāh ﷻ takes oath swearing by the prophets.
4) Allāh ﷻ takes oath swearing by the holy Qur'ān.

1. First Meaning: Allāh ﷻ takes oath by the wind. Each verse refers to a different type of wind:

	Verse:	Interpretation regarding winds:
1	وَالْمُرْسَلَٰتِ عُرْفًا	A breeze that is soft and provides comfort; adding tranquility to a person's environment.
2	فَالْعَٰصِفَٰتِ عَصْفًا	A violent wind that causes storms and hurricanes.
3	وَالنَّٰشِرَٰتِ نَشْرًا	A wind that gathers the clouds together to produce rain.
4	فَالْفَٰرِقَٰتِ فَرْقًا	This type of wind causes the clouds to break up and scatter.

Oaths in the First Five Verses of Sūrah Mursalāt (First Meaning)

5   فَالْمُلْقِيَاتِ ذِكْرًا

These winds inspire the dhikr of Allāh ﷻ. The winds will either be making an excuse for the people, i.e. repentance for the people who are righteous or serve as a warning to those who are heedless. If we take admonition from it, it will become 'udhr (repentance) but if we fail to act upon it, it will be nudhr (a warning):

عُذْرًا أَوْ نُذْرًا ۞

"Either (inspiring) repentance or caution." (77:6)

The holy Qur'ān itself is dhikr, as Allāh ﷻ says:

إِنَّا نَحْنُ نَزَّلْنَا الذِّكْرَ وَإِنَّا لَهُ لَحَافِظُونَ ۞

"Without doubt, We have revealed the Reminder and We shall certainly be its Protectors." (15:9)

All the prophets who were sent to this world were bashīr (a giver of glad tidings) and nadhīr (warner). They gave glad tidings to those who believed and accepted īmān, but those who refused to accept were given the warning of the severe punishment that lies in wait for them respectively.

After taking the oaths, Allāh ﷻ then says:

$$\text{إِنَّمَا تُوعَدُونَ لَوَاقِعٌ}$$

"Verily what you have been warned about (Day of Judgement) shall certainly take place." (77:7)

Allāh ﷻ takes five consecutive oaths to draw emphasis on the certainty of the Day of Judgement.

Just merely mentioning a certain point is enough for emphasis when the Lord of the worlds makes a statement. For Him to then take oaths and not just one, but five separate consecutive oaths in succession, is further emphasising the seriousness and gravity of the matter at hand.

2. Second Meaning: Allāh ﷻ takes oath by the angels i.e. each verse refer to the angel:

	Verse:	Interpretation regarding the angels:
1	وَالْمُرْسَلَاتِ عُرْفًا	Angels of mercy when they descend to extract the rūh (soul) from a body with compassion and gentleness.
2	فَالْعَاصِفَاتِ عَصْفًا	Angels who are very severe in bringing the punishment and chastisement. They rip the rūh out of the body in a very painful and excruciating manner

Oaths in the First Five Verses of Sūrah Mursalāt (Second Meaning)

3	وَالنَّاشِرَاتِ نَشْرًا	Angels who spread out the clouds and control whether it rains or not in accordance with Allāh's ﷻ order.
4	فَالْفَارِقَاتِ فَرْقًا	Angels who cause the clouds to break up and scatter.
5	فَالْمُلْقِيَاتِ ذِكْرًا	Angels which inspire the remembrance of Allāh ﷻ:

عُذْرًا أَوْ نُذْرًا ۞

"Either (inspiring) repentance or caution." (77:6)

Scholars say that these verses refer to Mīkā'īl ؑ as he oversees the winds and the changes in climate. Other scholars say that it refers to Isrāfīl ؑ. This is because when he will blow the trumpet the first time; everyone will be scattered and separated, and when he blows for the second time; everyone will be gathered and brought to account; in inducing Allāh's ﷻ remembrance to the reality of what will await them on that fateful day.

Many of the commentators say that these verses of Sūrah Mursalāt refer to Sayyidunā Jibrīl ؑ when he brought down the revelation to the different prophets.

When advice would come, the disbelievers would reject the message. On the Day of Judgement, they will beg and plead to be sent back so that they can make amends but their pleading will be of no avail:

رَبَّنَا أَخْرِجْنَا مِنْهَا فَإِنْ عُدْنَا فَإِنَّا ظَالِمُونَ ۝١٠٧ قَالَ اخْسَئُوا فِيهَا وَلَا تُكَلِّمُونِ ۝١٠٨

"O our Lord! Remove us from here (return us to the world)! If we ever repeat ourselves (by doing what we did previously in the world), then we must surely be oppressors. Allāh will say, 'Remain disgraced in it (Jahannam) and do not speak to Me!'" (23: 107-108)

When revelation descended, it provided the opportunity for the believers to make amends. For those who did not heed the message and persisted in turning away, Allāh ﷻ says:

وَلَنُذِيقَنَّهُم مِّنَ الْعَذَابِ الْأَدْنَىٰ دُونَ الْعَذَابِ الْأَكْبَرِ لَعَلَّهُمْ يَرْجِعُونَ ۝

"We shall definitely let them taste the closer (lesser) punishment (punishment in the world) before the greater punishment (in the Hereafter) so that they may return." (32:21)

Sometimes, when a person commits a sin, in order to bring them back on the right path, Allāh ﷻ may inflict them with a punishment which then compels a person to re-examine their lives and make the necessary changes in order to save themselves from the greater punishment in the Hereafter.

In another verse, Allāh ﷻ says:

إِنَّ بَطْشَ رَبِّكَ لَشَدِيدٌ ۝

Oaths in the First Five Verses of Sūrah Mursalāt (Third Meaning)

"Undoubtedly the grasp (punishment) of your Lord is severe indeed." (85:12)

3. Third Meaning: Allāh ﷻ takes oath by the prophets referring to their characteristics:

	Verse:	Interpretation regarding the prophets ﷺ:
1	وَٱلْمُرْسَلَٰتِ عُرْفًا	The kind and gentle nature of the prophets who were sent down in succession as and when the need arose to direct people towards guidance. They were sent for the spiritual prosperity and well-being of mankind.
2	فَٱلْعَٰصِفَٰتِ عَصْفًا	The firm and strict prophets like Sayyidunā Mūsā ﷺ. The severity of their anger was directed at uprooting evil, destroying the wrong beliefs and evil practices of the disbelievers.
3	وَٱلنَّٰشِرَٰتِ نَشْرًا	This refers to the proclamation of their message reaching far and wide.
4	فَٱلْفَٰرِقَٰتِ فَرْقًا	Through their da'wah (calling people to Islām), the people became separated into two groups: • those who accepted faith, • those who rejected faith.
5	فَٱلْمُلْقِيَٰتِ ذِكْرًا	The prophets reminded people regarding the importance of Allāh's ﷻ remembrance.

Through the prophets' message, the righteous people turned to Allāh ﷻ in repentance and the evil people were warned against committing sins.

4. Fourth Meaning: Allāh ﷻ **takes oath by the holy Qur'ān** i.e. Allāh ﷻ takes an oath, directly referring to the verses of the holy Qur'ān.

	Verse:	Interpretation regarding the holty Qur'ān:
1	وَالْمُرْسَلَاتِ عُرْفًا	This is regarding the verses that bring us glad tidings of benefit and happiness, i.e. those verses in the holy Qur'ān that will cause people to rejoice.
2	فَالْعَاصِفَاتِ عَصْفًا	These verses warn mankind that if they do not take heed and deny the true message, then there will be severe consequences.:

إِنَّ الَّذِينَ كَفَرُوا بِآيَاتِنَا سَوْفَ نُصْلِيهِمْ نَارًا كُلَّمَا نَضِجَتْ جُلُودُهُمْ بَدَّلْنَاهُمْ جُلُودًا غَيْرَهَا لِيَذُوقُوا الْعَذَابَ ۗ إِنَّ اللَّهَ كَانَ عَزِيزًا حَكِيمًا ۞

"Indeed, those who reject our āyāt (signs),
We shall soon enter them into the Fire.
Whenever their skins melt, We shall
exchange them for fresh skins so that they

Oaths in the First Five Verses of Sūrah Mursalāt (Fourth Meaning)

2		may taste the punishment. Undoubtedly, Allāh is Mighty, the Wise." (4:56)
		These type of verses are divided into two categories: 1. Those which explain about Jannah. 2. Those which describe the horrors of Jahannam.
3	وَٱلنَّٰشِرَٰتِ نَشْرًا	These verses stretch out in expounding on the articles of faith and all that is required of knowledge.
4	فَٱلْفَٰرِقَٰتِ فَرْقًا	These type of verse have been revealed to direct people towards guidance and divides people into two groups: 1. The people of Paradise. 2. The people of Hellfire. There are two categories of people; hizbullāh (group of Allāh ﷻ) and hizbushaytān (group of Shaytān). The hizbullāh will enter into Jannah and the hizbushaytān will enter the fire of Jahannam.
5	فَٱلْمُلْقِيَٰتِ ذِكْرًا	This refers to those verses which inspire the inspiration, i.e. those verses which inspire the dhikr of Allāh ﷻ.

Regarding the remembrance of Allāh ﷻ, we find verses such as:

$$\text{اَلَّذِيْنَ اٰمَنُوْا وَتَطْمَئِنُّ قُلُوْبُهُمْ بِذِكْرِ اللهِ ۗ اَلَا بِذِكْرِ اللهِ تَطْمَئِنُّ الْقُلُوْبُ}$$

"Those who have īmān and whose hearts are connected with the dhikr of Allāh. Behold! Hearts are contented with the dhikr of Allāh." (13:28)

$$\text{يٰٓاَيُّهَا الَّذِيْنَ اٰمَنُوا اذْكُرُوا اللهَ ذِكْرًا كَثِيْرًا ۝ وَسَبِّحُوْهُ بُكْرَةً وَّاَصِيْلًا ۝}$$

"O you have īmān! Remember Allāh in abundance and glorify Him morning and evening." (33:41-42)

By calling Allāh ﷻ in remembrance of Him, we are fulfilling the objective of life. This world is for us to take benefit from and to utilise our time in remembering His Majesty and Greatness, in all that He has endowed and bestowed upon us.

Why is mankind referred to as the best of creation? Because of his ability to differentiate between right and wrong:

$$\text{لَقَدْ خَلَقْنَا الْإِنْسَانَ فِيْٓ اَحْسَنِ تَقْوِيْمٍ}$$

"Undoubtedly, We created man in the best form." (95:4)

Every other living creature except jinn is devoid of the conscience of free will. Hence, mankind and jinn will be the only creation that will be taken to task from all the living creatures of the earth.

$$\text{عُذْرًا أَوْ نُذْرًا}$$

"Either (inspiring) repentance or caution." (77:6)

When a person reflects deeply and sincerely on the verses of the holy Qur'ān, it will cause a person to turn towards Allāh ﷻ in repentance. For those who choose to reject its message, then it will serve as a warning to them.

In light of all the meanings given above, the allegories used present a wide and all-embracing scope to interpret the first five verses Allāh ﷻ takes oath by.

$$\text{إِنَّمَا تُوعَدُونَ لَوَاقِعٌ}$$

"Verily what you have been warned about (Day of Judgement) shall certainly take place." (77:7)

In this verse, Allāh ﷻ puts forward the conviction of the Day of Judgement; the certainty that it will take place. This statement is made after Allāh ﷻ takes five oaths. The seriousness and gravity of this day is stressed through Allāh ﷻ taking these oaths because the disbelievers would jest and ridicule the holy Prophet ﷺ when he would explain about the reality of this day. The disbelievers would ask as to when this Day of Judgement would take place:

$$\text{وَيَقُولُونَ مَتَىٰ هَٰذَا الْوَعْدُ إِن كُنتُمْ صَادِقِينَ}$$

"They (the disbelievers) say, 'When will this promise (the Day of

Judgement) take place if you are truthful?" (67:25)

وَيَوْمَ نَبْعَثُ مِنْ كُلِّ أُمَّةٍ شَهِيدًا ثُمَّ لَا يُؤْذَنُ لِلَّذِيْنَ كَفَرُوْا وَلَا هُمْ يُسْتَعْتَبُوْنَ ۞

"The Day of Judgement when We shall raise a witness (a prophet) from every nation, then the disbelievers will not be granted permission (to make excuses for their behaviour), nor will they be allowed to please Allāh." (16:84)

وَأَتْبَعْنٰهُمْ فِىْ هٰذِهِ الدُّنْيَا لَعْنَةً ۖ وَيَوْمَ الْقِيٰمَةِ هُمْ مِّنَ الْمَقْبُوْحِيْنَ ۞

"We set a curse after them in this world and on the Day of Judgement they shall be among the despised ones." (28:42)

اَللّٰهُ لَا إِلٰهَ إِلَّا هُوَ ۚ لَيَجْمَعَنَّكُمْ إِلٰى يَوْمِ الْقِيٰمَةِ لَا رَيْبَ فِيْهِ ۗ وَمَنْ أَصْدَقُ مِنَ اللّٰهِ حَدِيْثًا ۞

"There is no god but Allāh. He will most definitely gather all of you one day about which there is no doubt. Who is it that speaks more truthfully than Allāh?" (4:87)

The Day of Judgement shall surely come, there is no doubt about it. The angel Sayyidunā Jibrīl ﷺ came disguised as a man and asked the holy Prophet ﷺ some questions regarding the religion. One of the questions he asked was:

فَأَخْبِرْنِيْ عَنِ السَّاعَةِ

"Inform me about the Hour."

The holy Prophet ﷺ replied:

$$\text{مَا الْمَسْئُوْلُ عَنْهَا بِأَعْلَمَ مِنَ السَّائِلِ}$$

"About that the one questioned knows no more than the questioner."

The holy Prophet ﷺ then mentioned some of the signs of the Day of Judgement and stated that it would be on a day which will correspond to a Friday.

Signs that will Commence the Day of Judgement

$$\text{وَإِذَا النُّجُومُ انْكَدَرَتْ}$$

"When the stars fall down (and cease to exist)." (81:2)

$$\text{إِذَا السَّمَآءُ انْفَطَرَتْ ۞ وَإِذَا الْكَوَاكِبُ انْتَثَرَتْ ۞}$$

"When the sky splits and when the stars fall." (82:1-2)

$$\text{فَإِذَا النُّجُومُ طُمِسَتْ ۞ وَإِذَا السَّمَآءُ فُرِجَتْ ۞}$$

"So when the light of the stars will be obliterated (extinguished). When the sky will be split (open up)." (77: 8-9)

This gives the impression that the gravitational force which keeps the stars in orbit will become affected, thereby causing the stars to fall out of alignment.

When a star is completely burnt out, it becomes a hunk of ash, which we refer to as a 'black dwarf'. The catastrophic changes which will take place prior to the commencement of the Day of Judgement, will cause all the stars to burn out.

If the gravitational force was abruptly increased by multiplying it by a given number, this would result in the stars burning out at a faster rate. And perhaps it is this force that Allāh ﷻ will assign to bring about the cataclysmic effects on the Day of Judgement. Allāh ﷻ knows best.

$$وَإِذَا الْجِبَالُ نُسِفَتْ$$

"When mountains will fly (move) about (tossed into the air by the violent convulsions of the earth)." (77:10)

$$وَيَسْأَلُونَكَ عَنِ الْجِبَالِ فَقُلْ يَنْسِفُهَا رَبِّي نَسْفًا ۝ فَيَذَرُهَا قَاعًا صَفْصَفًا ۝ لَا تَرَى فِيهَا عِوَجًا وَلَا أَمْتًا ۝$$

"They ask you (O Prophet) about the mountains. Say, 'My Lord shall completely remove them (shatter them to dust) leaving the earth as a barren (completely level) plain on which you will neither see any depressions nor any protrusions (with nothing sunken below or standing above the ground).'" (20: 105-107)

$$وَخَسَفَ الْقَمَرُ ۝ وَجُمِعَ الشَّمْسُ وَالْقَمَرُ ۝$$

"The moon will eclipse (lose its light). And the sun and moon will be joined." (75: 8-9)

When the gravitational force exceeds a certain limit, for example, if the force of gravity suddenly became ten times stronger, mountains would be too steep to hold up. When this happens, they would crumble into a massive movement of rock and dirt. The surface of the earth would also become much flatter. The trees would fall down. We would also become crushed as our capillaries would get destroyed, causing damage to our heart and organ system.

Allāh ﷻ alone knows what forces He will utilise in bringing about these effects. However, the fact that these forces exist in nature and we can predict the behaviour of such forces in the way they would affect our solar system, and then extrapolate them to fit the descriptions given in the holy Qur'ān of the behaviour of the planets and the stars, further highlights that this revelation could not have come from no other than that of a divine origin.

وَإِذَا الرُّسُلُ أُقِّتَتْ ۞

"And when the messengers (with their people) will be gathered for an appointed time." (77:11)

All the messengers will be gathered together at an appointed time and then will be questioned by Allāh ﷻ.

Sayyidunā Abdullāh ibn Mas'ūd ؓ narrates that the holy Prophet ﷺ said to him:

$$\text{اِقْرَأْ عَلَيَّ الْقُرْآنَ فَقُلْتُ يَا رَسُوْلَ اللهِ أَقْرَأُ عَلَيْكَ وَعَلَيْكَ أُنْزِلَ قَالَ إِنِّي أُحِبُّ أَنْ أَسْمَعَهُ مِنْ غَيْرِيْ فَقَرَأْتُ عَلَيْهِ سُوْرَةَ النِّسَاءِ حَتّٰى جِئْتُ إِلٰى هٰذِهِ الْآيَةِ فَكَيْفَ إِذَا جِئْنَا مِنْ كُلِّ أُمَّةٍ بِشَهِيْدٍ وَجِئْنَا بِكَ عَلٰى هٰؤُلَاءِ شَهِيْدًا قَالَ حَسْبُكَ الْآنَ فَالْتَفَتُّ إِلَيْهِ فَإِذَا عَيْنَاهُ تَذْرِفَانِ}$$

"Recite the holy Qur'ān for me." He said, "O Messenger of Allāh ﷺ! Should I recite to you and it was revealed to you?" He (the holy Prophet ﷺ) said, "Yes, for I like to hear it from others." "I recited Sūrah Nisā' until I reached the āyah: **How will it be when We shall bring forth a witness from every nation and call you (O Messenger of Allāh ﷺ) to be a witness over all of them?" (4:41)**. He (the holy Prophet ﷺ) then said, "Stop now." (Sayyidunā Abdullāh ibn Mas'ūd ؓ said), "I found that his eyes were tearful." (Bukhārī, Muslim)

The holy Prophet ﷺ was reflecting upon his beloved ummah; how he would have to stand witness against those who disobeyed. The holy Prophet's ﷺ desire was to see that each and every one of his ummah would enter Paradise.

When the following sūrah was revealed:

$$\text{وَالضُّحٰى ﴿١﴾ وَاللَّيْلِ إِذَا سَجٰى ﴿٢﴾ مَا وَدَّعَكَ رَبُّكَ وَمَا قَلٰى ﴿٣﴾ وَلَلْآخِرَةُ خَيْرٌ لَكَ مِنَ الْأُوْلٰى ﴿٤﴾ وَلَسَوْفَ يُعْطِيْكَ رَبُّكَ فَتَرْضٰى ﴿٥﴾}$$

"By the light of day! By the night when it settles! Your Lord has neither forsaken you (O Prophet) nor does He dislike you. The Hereafter is certainly much better for you than this world. Your Lord shall soon give you (an abundance of bounties in the

Hereafter) and you shall be pleased." (93: 1-5)

This sūrah gave the glad tidings that the holy Prophet ﷺ would be granted the ability to intercede for his ummah, and he will not feel content to see any member of his ummah in Jahannam (Hellfire). Although he will intercede for them, there will be those whom the holy Prophet ﷺ will be compelled to turn his face away from as a result of their practice of bid'ah – matters innovated in the dīn. The holy Prophet ﷺ will tell them to go away from him.

Sayyidunā Sahl ibn S`ad ؓ heard the holy Prophet ﷺ saying:

أَنَا فَرَطُكُمْ عَلَى الْحَوْضِ مَنْ وَرَدَ شَرِبَ وَمَنْ شَرِبَ لَمْ يَظْمَأْ أَبَدًا وَلَيَرِدَنَّ عَلَىَّ أَقْوَامٌ أَعْرِفُهُمْ وَيَعْرِفُوْنِيْ ثُمَّ يُحَالُ بَيْنِيْ وَبَيْنَهُمْ فَيَقُولُ إِنَّهُمْ مِنِّي فَيُقَالُ إِنَّكَ لَا تَدْرِيْ مَا عَمِلُوْا بَعْدَكَ فَأَقُوْلُ سُحْقًا سُحْقًا لِمَنْ بَدَّلَ بَعْدِيْ

"I will reach the cistern ahead of you. He who comes to me will drink, and whoever drinks will never be thirsty again. There will come to me some people whom I will recognise and they will recognise me, then they will be prevented from reaching me… I shall say, 'They are of me,' but it will be said, 'You do not know what they introduced after you were gone.' So, I shall say, 'Away, away with those who changed (the religion) after I was gone.'" (Muslim)

Those who committed bid'ah (innovation) will be turned away. These are the people with regards to whom the holy Qur'ān says:

Signs that will Commence the Day of Judgement

$$\text{وَقَالَ الرَّسُولُ يَٰرَبِّ إِنَّ قَوْمِي اتَّخَذُوا هَٰذَا الْقُرْآنَ مَهْجُورًا}$$

"(On the Day of Judgement) the Messenger will say, 'O my Lord! My people have ignored this Qur'ān.'" (25:30)

Allāh ﷻ will gather all the prophets on the Day of Judgement and they will be asked about how their respective nations responded to them. Every prophet delivered the message in warning the people. The prophets came to them people and invited them to Islām:

$$\text{إِنِّي لَكُمْ رَسُولٌ أَمِينٌ ۝ فَاتَّقُوا اللَّهَ وَأَطِيعُونِ ۝}$$

"I am certainly a trustworthy messenger to you. So, fear Allāh and obey me." (26: 125-126)

But these people denied the messengers. On the Day of Judgement, they will put forward their excuses, claiming that no one came to them. They will blatantly lie and say that no messenger had been sent to them. Allāh ﷻ will then turn to the messengers and ask what they had in response to this.

The prophets will bring forward the ummah of Muhammad ﷺ. It will be said that these people were not present at the time of the other prophets, so how would they be able to answer correctly? The ummah of Muhammad ﷺ will respond by saying that they read the holy Qur'ān and found all the other prophets that were sent mentioned in their holy Book.

Sayyidunā Nūh ﷺ for example, preached for 950 years in calling people to his message:

$$\text{وَلَقَدْ أَرْسَلْنَا نُوحًا إِلَىٰ قَوْمِهِ فَلَبِثَ فِيهِمْ أَلْفَ سَنَةٍ إِلَّا خَمْسِينَ عَامًا فَأَخَذَهُمُ ٱلطُّوفَانُ وَهُمْ ظَٰلِمُونَ ۝}$$

"Without doubt We sent Nūh (as a messenger) to his nation, where he remained (preaching the oneness of Allāh) for a thousand years less fifty years (950 years). Then a storm struck them while they were oppressive." (29:14)

$$\text{إِنَّا أَرْسَلْنَا نُوحًا إِلَىٰ قَوْمِهِ أَنْ أَنذِرْ قَوْمَكَ مِن قَبْلِ أَن يَأْتِيَهُمْ عَذَابٌ أَلِيمٌ ۝ قَالَ يَٰقَوْمِ إِنِّي لَكُمْ نَذِيرٌ مُّبِينٌ ۝ أَنِ ٱعْبُدُوا۟ ٱللَّهَ وَٱتَّقُوهُ وَأَطِيعُونِ ۝}$$

"Verily We sent Nūh (as a prophet) to his nation instructing him, 'Warn your people before a painful punishment afflicts them. He said, 'O my people! Indeed, I am a clear warner to you. Worship Allāh, fear Him and obey me.'" (71: 1-3)

However, the people were defiant and rejected his message. This is mentioned in the following verse:

$$\text{قَالَ رَبِّ إِنِّي دَعَوْتُ قَوْمِي لَيْلًا وَنَهَارًا ۝ فَلَمْ يَزِدْهُمْ دُعَآئِي إِلَّا فِرَارًا ۝}$$

"He said, 'O my Lord! Indeed, I called my people day and night. However, my calling only made them run further away.'" (71:5-6)

The ummah of the Prophet ﷺ will support the claim of the other prophets by saying that this was revealed in the holy Qur'ān. The holy Qur'ān which they read, was brought to them through the medium of their beloved Prophet Muhammad ﷺ.

The situation on that day will be so severe that whilst all the others will be calling out, "O Allāh, save me, save me!" there will be only one person who will be calling out on the contrary; "My ummah, my ummah!" And that will be our beloved Prophet Muhammad ﷺ. His entire life, his anxiousness was in worrying for his ummah. Many a times, Allāh ﷻ would console the holy Prophet ﷺ because of his excessive grief, on account of the people not accepting faith:

$$\text{فَلَعَلَّكَ بَاخِعٌ نَفْسَكَ عَلَىٰ آثَارِهِمْ إِنْ لَمْ يُؤْمِنُوا بِهَٰذَا الْحَدِيثِ أَسَفًا}$$

"It should not be that you (O Prophet) destroy yourself in grief after them because they do not believe in this communication (holy Qur'ān)." (18:6)

$$\text{لَقَدْ جَاءَكُمْ رَسُولٌ مِنْ أَنْفُسِكُمْ عَزِيزٌ عَلَيْهِ مَا عَنِتُّمْ حَرِيصٌ عَلَيْكُمْ بِالْمُؤْمِنِينَ رَءُوفٌ رَّحِيمٌ}$$

"Undoubtedly, a Messenger from yourselves has come to you. The difficulties that afflict you are very distressing to him. He is anxious for (good to come to) you and extremely forgiving and merciful towards the believers." (9:128)

Abū Jahl was a staunch enemy of the holy Prophet ﷺ. He would say,

"If this religion is correct, then send upon us a rain of stones or bring down a severe punishment." This matter would have already been settled had it not been for the Day of Judgement, as Allāh ﷻ states:

$$\text{لِأَيِّ يَوْمٍ أُجِّلَتْ ﴿١٢﴾ لِيَوْمِ الْفَصْلِ ﴿١٣﴾}$$

"For which day shall their matter (the punishment of the disbelievers) be postponed? For the Day of Judgement." (77:12-13)

$$\text{وَلَوْ يُؤَاخِذُ اللهُ النَّاسَ بِظُلْمِهِم مَّا تَرَكَ عَلَيْهَا مِن دَابَّةٍ وَلَٰكِن يُؤَخِّرُهُمْ إِلَىٰ أَجَلٍ مُّسَمًّى ۖ فَإِذَا جَاءَ أَجَلُهُمْ لَا يَسْتَأْخِرُونَ سَاعَةً وَلَا يَسْتَقْدِمُونَ}$$

"If Allāh were to take people to task for their injustice, He would not have left a single creature on earth, but He grants them respite until an appointed term. When their term expires, they will not be able to delay it for a moment, nor bring it forward." (16:61)

$$\text{مَٰلِكِ يَوْمِ الدِّينِ}$$

"And Master of the Day of Recompense." (1:3)

Allāh ﷻ is the Master of the Day of Judgement. He will place the people into different groups. This is mentioned in the following verse:

$$\text{وَامْتَازُوا الْيَوْمَ أَيُّهَا الْمُجْرِمُونَ}$$

"Separate yourselves (from the believers) today, O you

criminals!" (36:59)

One of the names given to the Day of Judgement is يَوْمُ الْفَضْل (yawmul fasl) – the day of differentiating between right and wrong. This is the day when the righteous people will be rewarded and those who were astray will be brought to account.

For example, Sayyidunā Nūh ﷺ continuously gave da'wah (invitation) in the hope that the people would accept the message but the people demanded that he brought down the punishment that he was threatening them with; if what he was saying was true:

$$\text{قَالُوا يَا نُوحُ قَدْ جَادَلْتَنَا فَأَكْثَرْتَ جِدَالَنَا فَأْتِنَا بِمَا تَعِدُنَا إِنْ كُنْتَ مِنَ الصَّادِقِينَ ﴿٣٢﴾ قَالَ إِنَّمَا يَأْتِيكُمْ بِهِ اللَّهُ إِنْ شَاءَ وَمَا أَنْتُمْ بِمُعْجِزِينَ ﴿٣٣﴾ وَلَا يَنْفَعُكُمْ نُصْحِي إِنْ أَرَدْتُ أَنْ أَنْصَحَ لَكُمْ إِنْ كَانَ اللَّهُ يُرِيدُ أَنْ يُغْوِيَكُمْ ۚ هُوَ رَبُّكُمْ وَإِلَيْهِ تُرْجَعُونَ ﴿٣٤﴾}$$

"They said, 'O Nūh! You have disputed with us and disputed to a great extent. So, bring forth what (punishment) you promised us if you are of the truthful ones.' He said, 'Only Allāh will bring it (the punishment) if He wills, and (when it comes) you will be unable to escape. My advice to you shall not benefit you if I intend to advise you while Allāh intends to send you astray (allows you to stray). He is your Lord and to Him shall you be returned.'" (11: 32-34)

The people would doubt the message that Sayyidunā Nūh ﷺ brought.

Many of the disbelievers would attempt to stop the prophets from delivering their message, and go as far as forcefully placing their hands over their mouths in an attempt to muffle their voices.

$$\text{لَقَدْ أَرْسَلْنَا نُوحًا إِلَىٰ قَوْمِهِ فَقَالَ يَا قَوْمِ اعْبُدُوا اللَّهَ مَا لَكُم مِّنْ إِلَٰهٍ غَيْرُهُ إِنِّي أَخَافُ عَلَيْكُمْ عَذَابَ يَوْمٍ عَظِيمٍ ﴿٥٩﴾ قَالَ الْمَلَأُ مِن قَوْمِهِ إِنَّا لَنَرَاكَ فِي ضَلَالٍ مُّبِينٍ ﴿٦٠﴾}$$

"Undoubtedly, We sent Nūh to his nation and he told them, 'O my people, worship only Allāh. There is no god for you besides Him. I fear the punishment of a great day for you.' The leaders of his people said (to him), 'We see that you are obviously deviated.'" (7: 59-60)

Sayyidunā Nūh ﷺ would not allow his anger to arise from within, but would reply to them in a calm manner:

$$\text{قَالَ يَا قَوْمِ لَيْسَ بِي ضَلَالَةٌ وَلَٰكِنِّي رَسُولٌ مِّن رَّبِّ الْعَالَمِينَ}$$

"He (Nūh) said, 'O my people! There is no deviation with me. On the contrary, I am a messenger from the Lord of the universe.'" (7:61)

Sayyidunā Nūh ﷺ then continued on in explaining to the people:

$$\text{أُبَلِّغُكُمْ رِسَالَاتِ رَبِّي وَأَنصَحُ لَكُمْ وَأَعْلَمُ مِنَ اللَّهِ مَا لَا تَعْلَمُونَ ﴿٦٢﴾ أَوَعَجِبْتُمْ أَن جَاءَكُمْ ذِكْرٌ مِّن رَّبِّكُمْ عَلَىٰ رَجُلٍ مِّنكُمْ لِيُنذِرَكُمْ وَلِتَتَّقُوا وَلَعَلَّكُمْ تُرْحَمُونَ ﴿٦٣﴾}$$

"I convey to you the messages of my Lord; advise you and I know things from Allāh about which you have no knowledge.

Are you surprised that a reminder from your Lord should come to you through a man from among you, so that he may warn you, so that you may fear (His punishment) and so that mercy may be shown to you?" (7: 62-63)

During the time of Sayyidunā Sālih ﷺ; after the people failed to take heed of the warning, they were also met with destruction. Looking at the remnants which were left behind after his people were destroyed, he said that no matter how much he had attempted in repeatedly advising them, the people had failed to listen. Thus, the punishment unleashed against them was justified:

فَأَخَذَتْهُمُ الرَّجْفَةُ فَأَصْبَحُوا فِي دَارِهِمْ جَٰثِمِينَ ﴿٧٨﴾ فَتَوَلَّىٰ عَنْهُمْ وَقَالَ يَٰقَوْمِ لَقَدْ أَبْلَغْتُكُمْ رِسَالَةَ رَبِّي وَنَصَحْتُ لَكُمْ وَلَٰكِن لَّا تُحِبُّونَ النَّٰصِحِينَ ﴿٧٩﴾

"So, an earthquake seized them and they lay face down (disgraced) in their homes (which were built to resist earthquakes). Sālih turned away from them and (addressing the dead nation) said, 'O my people! I conveyed to you the message of my Lord and advised you, but you seemed not to like advisors.'" (7:78-79)

When Sayyidunā Hūd ﷺ preached the message of tawhīd, the people would turn to him and say that he was a lunatic. He however, would remain composed and calm in responding to their disapproval:

$$\text{وَإِلَىٰ عَادٍ أَخَاهُمْ هُودًا ۗ قَالَ يَٰقَوْمِ ٱعْبُدُوا۟ ٱللَّهَ مَا لَكُم مِّنْ إِلَٰهٍ غَيْرُهُۥ ۚ أَفَلَا تَتَّقُونَ ﴿٦٥﴾ قَالَ ٱلْمَلَأُ ٱلَّذِينَ كَفَرُوا۟ مِن قَوْمِهِۦٓ إِنَّا لَنَرَىٰكَ فِى سَفَاهَةٍ وَإِنَّا لَنَظُنُّكَ مِنَ ٱلْكَٰذِبِينَ ﴿٦٦﴾ قَالَ يَٰقَوْمِ لَيْسَ بِى سَفَاهَةٌ وَلَٰكِنِّى رَسُولٌ مِّن رَّبِّ ٱلْعَٰلَمِينَ ﴿٦٧﴾}$$

"To the nation of ʿĀd, We sent their brother Hūd. He told them, 'O my people! Worship only Allāh. There is no god for you besides Him. Do you not fear (His punishment)?' The leaders of his nation who disbelieved said, 'Indeed we see you (drowning) in foolishness and we surely consider you to be among the liars.' He said, 'O my people! There is no foolishness with me. On the contrary, I am a messenger from the Lord of the universe.'" (7:65-67)

This is also teaching us that when we propagate the message of Islām, we must do so in a gentle and forbearing manner without being merciless and harsh.

Once a person set off to give da'wah to a ruler of a kingdom. He began to put his message across in a very harsh manner. The ruler interrupted him saying, "You are not better than Sayyidunā Mūsā عليه السلام and I am not as evil as Fir'awn!"

When Allāh ﷻ sent Sayyidunā Mūsā عليه السلام to Fir'awn, He commanded him to speak to Fir'awn in a compassionate way.

$$\text{فَقُولَا لَهُۥ قَوْلًا لَّيِّنًا لَّعَلَّهُۥ يَتَذَكَّرُ أَوْ يَخْشَىٰ}$$

"Speak to him in gentle (kind) words, perchance he may take

heed or fear (Me)." (20:44)

$$\text{يَسْأَلُونَكَ عَنِ السَّاعَةِ أَيَّانَ مُرْسَاهَا ۖ قُلْ إِنَّمَا عِلْمُهَا عِندَ رَبِّي ۖ لَا يُجَلِّيهَا لِوَقْتِهَا إِلَّا هُوَ ۚ ثَقُلَتْ فِي السَّمَاوَاتِ وَالْأَرْضِ ۚ لَا تَأْتِيكُمْ إِلَّا بَغْتَةً ۗ يَسْأَلُونَكَ كَأَنَّكَ حَفِيٌّ عَنْهَا ۖ قُلْ إِنَّمَا عِلْمُهَا عِندَ اللَّهِ وَلَٰكِنَّ أَكْثَرَ النَّاسِ لَا يَعْلَمُونَ}$$

"They ask you (O Prophet of Allāh) about the Day of Judgement, when will it occur? Say, 'The knowledge of this is with my Lord. Only He will make it appear on its time. It (the occurrence of the Day of Judgement) will be weighty on the heavens and the earth and will appear suddenly.' They ask you as if you have perfect knowledge of it. Say, 'The knowledge of this is only with Allāh, but most people do not know.'" (7:187)

Allāh ﷻ asks – do you know what the Day of Judgement is?

$$\text{وَمَا أَدْرَاكَ مَا يَوْمُ الْفَصْلِ}$$

"What will tell you what the Day of Judgement is?" (77:14)

It will be destruction on that day for those who were the deniers of faith.

$$\text{وَيْلٌ يَوْمَئِذٍ لِّلْمُكَذِّبِينَ}$$

"May misery be the end of the rejecters (of the Day of Judgement) on that day!" (77:15)

The Arabic word 'وَيْلٌ' ('waylun') used in this verse refers to 'destruction' which will occur on those who refused to believe in the message.

Other scholars have said that 'وَيْلٌ' refers to a valley in Jahannam, which is so fierce that even the people of Jahannam ask refuge in Allāh ﷻ to be protected from this valley. This valley oozes pus, blood and the sweat of the people of Jahannam.

Those that had rejected faith will wish that they had been believers but, on that day, it will be too late to declare their acceptance of belief.

Allāh ﷻ says:

رُّبَمَا يَوَدُّ ٱلَّذِينَ كَفَرُوا لَوْ كَانُوا مُسْلِمِينَ ۞

"Many a time (on the Day of Judgement) the disbelievers will wish that they were Muslims." (15:2)

وَكَانَ يَوْمًا عَلَى ٱلْكَافِرِينَ عَسِيرًا ۞

"The day will be very difficult for the disbelievers." (25:26)

This will be because on this day, they will receive the judgement of being condemned to Hellfire for eternity.

After the last Prophet was sent, the only religion acceptable in the court of Allāh ﷻ is Islām. The holy Qur'ān says:

﴿ إِنَّ الدِّينَ عِندَ اللهِ الْإِسْلَامُ ﴾

"Definitely, the only religion with Allāh (acceptable to Allāh) is Islām." (3:19)

﴿ وَمَنْ يَبْتَغِ غَيْرَ الْإِسْلَامِ دِينًا فَلَنْ يُقْبَلَ مِنْهُ وَهُوَ فِي الْآخِرَةِ مِنَ الْخَاسِرِينَ ﴾

"Whoever seeks a religion besides Islām, it shall never be accepted from him and he will be among the losers in the Hereafter." (3:85)

Regarding those who act according to their own whims and desires, Allāh ﷻ says:

﴿ وَقَدِمْنَا إِلَىٰ مَا عَمِلُوا مِنْ عَمَلٍ فَجَعَلْنَاهُ هَبَاءً مَّنْثُورًا ﴾

"We will then turn (Our attention) to their (good) deeds and reduce them to scattered dust (render them worthless because they were carried out without īmān)." (25:23)

There will be no weighing as their good deeds will become obliterated. Allāh ﷻ is Just, so whatever good they carried out in the world will be recompensed in this life, but in the Ākhirah there will be no reward for them.

﴿ الَّذِينَ يَقُولُونَ رَبَّنَا إِنَّنَا آمَنَّا فَاغْفِرْ لَنَا ذُنُوبَنَا وَقِنَا عَذَابَ النَّارِ ﴾

"Those who say, 'O our Lord, we certainly have īmān (faith), so forgive our sins and save us from the punishment of the fire.'" (3:16)

Scholars have said that the Arabic letter 'ف' ('fā') in 'فَاغْفِرْ لَنَا' ('faghfirlanā') follows after the word 'اِيْمَان' ('īmān'). This means that a prerequisite of being forgiven is that a person must have īmān prior to being forgiven.

$$ اَلَمْ نُهْلِكِ الْاَوَّلِيْنَ ۝ ثُمَّ نُتْبِعُهُمُ الْاٰخِرِيْنَ ۝ كَذٰلِكَ نَفْعَلُ بِالْمُجْرِمِيْنَ ۝ وَيْلٌ يَّوْمَئِذٍ لِّلْمُكَذِّبِيْنَ ۝ $$

"Have We not destroyed the former nations and then joined the later generations with them (by destroying them as well)? Thus, do We treat the criminals. May misery be the end of the rejecters on that day! (77: 16-19)

The disbelievers would ask the holy Prophet ﷺ as to why no punishment had descended upon them, since they had disbelieved in his message. Allāh ﷻ pre-warns them in this verse that He had destroyed the previous nations because of their disbelief and also the later generations that had followed in their footsteps.

The qawm (nation) of Ād, the qawm of Thamūd, the qawm of Sayyidunā Nūh عليه السلام, the qawm of Sayyidunā Shu'ayb عليه السلام, Fir'awn and his followers; all of them were destroyed. Even until this day, the remnants of many of the places where these people once dwelled and lodged remain preserved. And many people visit these sites as a sign of taking admonishment.

Signs that will Commence the Day of Judgement

Sayyidunā Ibn Umar ؓ mentioned that when the holy Prophet ﷺ passed by Al-Hijr – which was the dwelling place of Thamūd, he said:

$$\text{لَا تَدْخُلُوا مَسَاكِنَ الَّذِينَ ظَلَمُوا أَنْفُسَهُمْ أَنْ يُّصِيْبَكُمْ مَا أَصَابَهُمْ إِلَّا أَنْ تَكُوْنُوا بَاكِيْنَ ثُمَّ قَنَّعَ رَأْسَهُ وَأَسْرَعَ السَّيْرَ حَتّٰى أَجَازَ الْوَادِيَ}$$

"Do not enter the dwelling places of those who wrong themselves, lest there befall you what befell them, unless you are weeping. Then he covered his head and hastened until he left the valley." (Bukhārī)

These people were destroyed because of their disobedience and rebellion against the prophets.

Our Shaykh mentioned on a lighter note about an incident where the imām was reciting Sūrah Mursalāt in his tarāwīh prayer. A bedouin was standing in the first saff (row) of prayer. When the imām recited the verse:

$$\text{أَلَمْ نُهْلِكِ الْأَوَّلِيْنَ}$$

"Have We not destroyed the former nations." (77:16)

The bedouin took this to mean the first row, so he immediately moved himself to the back row, fearing that he might be met with destruction. Then the imām recited the next verse:

$$\text{ثُمَّ نُتْبِعُهُمُ الْآخِرِينَ}$$

"And then joined the later generations with them (by destroying them as well)?" (77:17)

He felt that this was referring to the back row he was standing in, so the man immediately broke his prayer and began running out of the masjid. As he was running, he heard the imām reciting the next verse:

$$\text{كَذَٰلِكَ نَفْعَلُ بِالْمُجْرِمِينَ}$$

"Thus do We treat the criminals." (77:18)

The person himself was called mujrimīn (criminals) so he said to himself, "He is indeed a magician (referring to the imām)."

Once, another bedouin was standing behind the imām whilst he began the recitation of Sūrah Baqarah. After finishing the prayer, the bedouin thought to himself, "If the imām makes his prayer this long next time, I will just leave the prayer!" He then spoke to the imām saying, "You read such a long sūrah, please could you read a short sūrah next time?" Hence in the next salāh the imām began reciting Sūrah Fīl. When the imām reached the word 'fīl', the man thought to himself that since this sūrah is named after an elephant, then it would be even greater in length than the previous sūrah which was named after a cow, hence, he immediately broke his prayer and left!

Another imām was reciting some verses regarding bedouins being severe in their kufr (disbelief) and nifāq (hypocrisy).

$$\text{ٱلْأَعْرَابُ أَشَدُّ كُفْرًا وَنِفَاقًا وَأَجْدَرُ أَلَّا يَعْلَمُوا حُدُودَ مَا أَنزَلَ ٱللَّهُ عَلَىٰ رَسُولِهِ ۗ وَٱللَّهُ عَلِيمٌ حَكِيمٌ ۝ وَمِنَ ٱلْأَعْرَابِ مَن يَتَّخِذُ مَا يُنفِقُ مَغْرَمًا وَيَتَرَبَّصُ بِكُمُ ٱلدَّوَائِرَ ۚ عَلَيْهِمْ دَائِرَةُ ٱلسَّوْءِ ۗ وَٱللَّهُ سَمِيعٌ عَلِيمٌ ۝}$$

> "The villagers (the desert Arabs) are extremely staunch in (committed to) disbelief and hypocrisy and are more likely to be ignorant of the limits that Allāh has revealed to His Messenger. Allāh is All-Knowing, The Wise. Among the villagers are those who consider what they spend (charity and contributions to jihād) as a tax (burden) and they await the ill-fortunes of fate to befall you (Muslims)." (9: 97-98)

The bedouin thought to himself, "He is talking about us!" He went behind the imām and struck him with a stick. After the imām had recovered, he came once again to lead the salāh. This time, he was reciting the verse about the bedouins who believe in Allāh ﷻ and the Last Day and spend in the path of Allāh ﷻ.

$$\text{وَمِنَ ٱلْأَعْرَابِ مَن يُؤْمِنُ بِٱللَّهِ وَٱلْيَوْمِ ٱلْآخِرِ وَيَتَّخِذُ مَا يُنفِقُ قُرُبَاتٍ عِندَ ٱللَّهِ وَصَلَوَاتِ ٱلرَّسُولِ ۚ أَلَا إِنَّهَا قُرْبَةٌ لَّهُمْ ۚ سَيُدْخِلُهُمُ ٱللَّهُ فِي رَحْمَتِهِ ۗ إِنَّ ٱللَّهَ غَفُورٌ رَّحِيمٌ ۝}$$

> "Among the villagers there are those who believe in Allāh and the Last Day. They consider what they spend as a means to gaining nearness to Allāh and the prayers of the Messenger. Behold! It will be a means of gaining nearness (and prayers) for

them. Allāh will soon enter them in His mercy. Undoubtedly, Allah is Most Forgiving, Most Merciful." (9:99)

After hearing this the bedouin said, "Now you have become right!" These were the simple-minded bedouins who took the literal approach in making sense of things.

Creation of Man

$$\text{أَلَمْ نَخْلُقكُّم مِّن مَّآءٍ مَّهِينٍ ﴿٢٠﴾ فَجَعَلْنَاهُ فِي قَرَارٍ مَّكِينٍ ﴿٢١﴾ إِلَىٰ قَدَرٍ مَّعْلُومٍ ﴿٢٢﴾ فَقَدَرْنَا فَنِعْمَ الْقَادِرُونَ ﴿٢٣﴾ وَيْلٌ يَوْمَئِذٍ لِّلْمُكَذِّبِينَ ﴿٢٤﴾}$$

"Have We not created you (man) from despised water (semen), placed it (the sperm) in a safe place (the womb) for a specified period and arranged (everything to perfection)? We are certainly the best of those who make arrangements. May misery be the end of the rejecters on that day!" (77: 20-24)

'Despised water' here, refers to the semen and the safe place makes reference to the mother's womb. The sperm fuses with the ovum and fertilisation takes place to produce an embryo, which then grows into a human being. This then remains in the mother's womb for just over nine months before the child is born into this world.

Allāh ﷻ says that He has made all the preparations and arrangements for the duration of stay in the mother's womb and also when the child is born into this world.

Creation of Man

These verses are specifically referring to those who deny the existence of Allāh ﷻ. Those who claim that after the Big-Bang, everything just came to be without there being any other external influence or any greater power behind it.

The Arabic word 'مَهِين' (mahīn) means something which is very lowly; despised. The semen; if it touches a person's body or clothes, it becomes impure. From this debased mixture, Allāh ﷻ brings about the best of creation. Allāh ﷻ says:

$$لَقَدْ خَلَقْنَا الْإِنْسَانَ فِي أَحْسَنِ تَقْوِيمٍ$$

"Undoubtedly, We created man in the best form." (95:4)

$$يَخْلُقُكُمْ فِي بُطُونِ أُمَّهَاتِكُمْ خَلْقًا مِنْ بَعْدِ خَلْقٍ فِي ظُلُمَاتٍ ثَلَاثٍ ۚ ذَٰلِكُمُ اللَّهُ رَبُّكُمْ لَهُ الْمُلْكُ ۖ لَا إِلَٰهَ إِلَّا هُوَ ۖ فَأَنَّىٰ تُصْرَفُونَ$$

"Allāh creates you in the wombs of your mothers, as a creation after creation in three (layers of) darkness. That is Allāh, your Lord, to Whom all kingdoms belong. There is none worthy of worship but Him, so where are you turning to?" (39:6)

The layers of darkness refer to the abdomen, the uterine wall and the placenta and its membrane in which the foetus develops.

During the first 40 days, the fertilised egg is a ball of cells splitting into the embryo and placenta. At 40 days, the embryo is the size of a small pea. After this stage, the embryo resembles a clot of blood.

Creation of Man

Thereafter, the clot becomes a body clothed with flesh. After four months, the soul enters the foetus and the organs and all the different parts of the body further mature into taking their respective roles and functions. All these things originated from impure semen.

Imagine a good cook who does not have the right ingredients to produce a certain dish that is required, or has ingredients of very inferior and poor quality. The dish they will produce will not taste to the specified expectation because of the low quality of ingredients, despite all the effort a person puts in to make the dish taste to the highest of standards. On the other hand, Allāh ﷻ creates the best of creation from the lowest form of substance.

The sperm and the egg cell; after fusing together, lodges itself in the mother's womb. It then resembles three stages of development in its appearance:

- نُطْفَة (nutfah) - drop
- عَلَقَة (alaqah) - leech-like structure
- مُضْغَة (mudghah) - chewed-like substance

The verse ends with Allāh ﷻ saying, **"so where are you turning to?"** This is similar to the example of how a loving father would address his son to come to the masjid when he is refusing to do so.

Allāh ﷻ says in the holy Qur'ān:

وَلَقَدْ خَلَقْنَا الْإِنسَانَ مِن سُلَالَةٍ مِّن طِينٍ ﴿١٢﴾ ثُمَّ جَعَلْنَاهُ نُطْفَةً فِي قَرَارٍ مَّكِينٍ ﴿١٣﴾ ثُمَّ

Creation of Man

$$\text{خَلَقْنَا النُّطْفَةَ عَلَقَةً فَخَلَقْنَا الْعَلَقَةَ مُضْغَةً فَخَلَقْنَا الْمُضْغَةَ عِظَامًا فَكَسَوْنَا الْعِظَامَ لَحْمًا ثُمَّ أَنْشَأْنَاهُ خَلْقًا آخَرَ ۚ فَتَبَارَكَ اللَّهُ أَحْسَنُ الْخَالِقِينَ ﴿١٤﴾}$$

"We have certainly created man (Ādam) from a product of (specially selected) clay. Thereafter, We placed him in a safe lodging (the womb) as a drop of fluid. Thereafter, We made the drop of fluid into a clot of blood, then the clot of blood into a lump of flesh, then the lump of flesh into bones, after which We dressed the bones in flesh. Thereafter, We made him into another type of creation. So blessed is Allāh, the Best of all creators." (23: 12-14)

The minimum gestational period is six months. In the days before the advancement of modern technology, in normal circumstances, a baby born after a gestational period of six months would have most likely struggled to survive. This is due to the difficulty of breathing unassisted on its own.

If a person had given birth to a healthy baby just five months after their marriage for example, then questions would have been raised about the identity of the father, because it would not have been possible to give birth to a healthy baby which would be developed enough to survive without the intervention of external medical equipment. Thus, if a woman gave birth after five months to a healthy baby who had no problems breathing, then serious questions would naturally be raised because it would be impossible for a baby at this stage to have developed this far. This would have pointed to conception taking place earlier (i.e. before marriage), and hence, paternity issues arising regarding the identity of the father.

However, in light of scientific advancement, the availability of paternity tests can also help eliminate any doubt or confusion, should any arise. In the previous eras where no such thing existed, the defining point in determining the father of a child would have been deduced when a woman would have been married to a man for at least six months; if she had given birth after six months of marriage. If she has given birth to a healthy viable infant before this minimum amount of time, then the lineage of the child would have naturally be put into question because a baby could not be fully developed in supporting itself before at least this minimum age, which itself would be a very delicate time in the uncertainty of the survival of the child.

1400 years ago, when the minimum age of pregnancy was stated as six months in the holy Qur'ān; the babies born during this age would have struggled to survive because of their premature births, so survival would have been a small number. However, by Allāh ﷻ placing the age of the gestational period to be a minimum of six months, indirectly points to and suggests that a time would come where a baby would be able to survive being born, even as early as this time.

A baby born after a gestational period of six months after the immediate marriage of a couple can only be attributed to a certain father. At this stage, it is developed enough to be a viable. This fact is supported with the advancement in Science where there is a 'general agreement' that babies born at 25 weeks onwards can survive, and that 'active management should be offered' to babies who are born at this premature age.

$$\text{وَاللَّهُ أَخْرَجَكُم مِّنْ بُطُونِ أُمَّهَٰتِكُمْ لَا تَعْلَمُونَ شَيْئًا وَجَعَلَ لَكُمُ ٱلسَّمْعَ وَٱلْأَبْصَٰرَ وَٱلْأَفْـِٔدَةَ لَعَلَّكُمْ تَشْكُرُونَ ۞}$$

"Allāh removed you from the wombs of your mothers when you knew nothing and blessed you with ears, eyes and hearts so that you may be grateful." (16:78)

Allāh ﷻ reminds us of our origins by saying:

$$\text{هَلْ أَتَىٰ عَلَى ٱلْإِنسَٰنِ حِينٌ مِّنَ ٱلدَّهْرِ لَمْ يَكُن شَيْـًٔا مَّذْكُورًا ۞}$$

"Undoubtedly, a moment in time has passed by man when he was not even something worth mentioning." (76:1)

The Punishment of Disbelief

The verse **"May misery be the end of the rejecters on that day!"** is mentioned ten times in Sūrah Mursalāt. Why has Allāh ﷻ laid emphasis on this point so much? Why did Allāh ﷻ not say this nine times or eleven times for example; why did He choose this specific number? Scholars of tafsīr have said regarding this verse that as Allāh ﷻ has given a human being intellect to differentiate between good and evil; this innate faculty compels us to believe in the existence of a creator. When a person destroys this capability through constant sinning, the recognition of this is taken away.

A person commits a sin for ten different reasons, and for each of them Allāh ﷻ says, **"May misery be the end of the rejecters on that day!"**

Quwwat-e-Nazriyyah

A person has the ability to understand the beliefs but denies them by denying the following six different things:

1) They deny the existence of God.
2) A person denies the sifāt (qualities) of Allāh ﷻ. They believe in Allāh ﷻ but ascribe God-like qualities with others, for example, believing that others have the power of forgiving or believing that the sun or moon has supernatural powers of helping them.
3) A person rejects the belief in the angels. The disbelievers at the time of the holy Prophet ﷺ would say that that angels were the daughters of Allāh ﷻ.

$$\text{وَيَجْعَلُونَ لِلَّهِ الْبَنَاتِ سُبْحَانَهُ وَلَهُم مَّا يَشْتَهُونَ}$$

"They ascribe daughters to Allāh. Allāh is pure! Yet they have for themselves what they desire." (16:57)

4) A person denies the Day of Judgement; they do not believe in

life after death.

5) A person does not believe in taqdīr (predestination).

6) A person rejects the messengers and books of Allāh ﷻ.

Quwwat-e-Shahwiyyah

This is the impulse to fulfil a person's desires. This is of two types: Ifrāt and Tafrīt.

- Quwwat-e-Shahwiyyah of Ifrāt – this is when a person's desires go beyond the limits in such a way that they reach a stage where they are perceived as being worse than animals. For example, a person commits acts of bestiality. Shāh Waliullāh Muhaddith Dehlawī ؒ writes in Hujjatullāhil-Bālighah, "Man will lose his natural instinct, he will become like an animal, he will do acts like an animal, and even commit acts worse than that of animals."
- Quwwat-e- Shahwiyyah of Tafrīt – a person makes harām that which Allāh ﷻ has made halāl and vice versa.

Quwwat-e-Ghadhabiyyah

This is also of two types: Ifrāt and Tafrīt.

1. Quwwat-e-Ghadhabiyyah of Ifrāt – when a person's anger goes beyond limits in such a way that it leads to tyranny and

oppression.

2. Quwwat-e-Ghadhabiyyah of Tafrīt – When a person never gets angry which results in many acts of evil being committed, with themselves turning a blind eye to it.

A person should only allow their anger to arise for the sake of Allāh ﷻ. Sayyidunā Abū Umāmah ؓ reports from the Messenger of Allāh ﷺ who stated:

$$\text{مَنْ أَحَبَّ لِلَّهِ وَأَبْغَضَ لِلَّهِ وَأَعْطَى لِلَّهِ وَمَنَعَ لِلَّهِ فَقَدِ اسْتَكْمَلَ الْإِيْمَانَ}$$

"Whoever loves for the sake of Allāh ﷻ, hates for the sake of Allāh ﷻ, gives for the sake of Allāh ﷻ and withholds for the sake of Allāh ﷻ has perfected the faith." (Abū Dāwūd)

In another hadīth, the Messenger of Allāh ﷺ said:

$$\text{أَفْضَلُ الْأَعْمَالِ الْحُبُّ فِي اللهِ وَالْبُغْضُ فِي اللهِ}$$

"The best of actions is to love for the sake of Allāh ﷻ and to hate for the sake of Allāh ﷻ." (Abū Dāwūd)

Hakīmul Ummah Shaykh Ashraf Alī Thānwī ؒ says that once he was disciplining a student when the student burst into tears and said, "Forgive me for the sake of Allāh ﷻ!" Shaykh Thānwī ؒ replied, "For the sake of Allāh ﷻ, I am disciplining you!"

How beautiful the Qur'ān is! Imām Ibn Kathīr ؒ mentions in his tafsīr saying,

$$\text{اُنْزِلَ أَشْرَفُ الْكُتُبِ بِأَشْرَفِ اللُّغَاتِ عَلٰى أَشْرَفِ الرُّسُلِ بِسِفَارَةِ أَشْرَفِ الْمَلَائِكَةِ وَكَانَ اِبْتِدَاءُ نُزُوْلِهٖ فِيْ أَشْرَفِ بِقَاعِ الْأَرْضِ وَهُوَ فِيْ أَشْرَفِ شُهُوْرِ السَّنَةِ وَهُوَ رَمَضَانُ فَكَمُلَ مِنْ كُلِّ الْوُجُوْهِ}$$

"The most noble Book (i.e. the holy Qur'ān) has been revealed in the most noble of languages (i.e. Arabic), upon His most noble of Prophets (i.e. Muhammad ﷺ), in the best of all lands (i.e. Makkah Mukarramah), through the medium of the best of angels (i.e. Sayyidunā Jibrīl علیہ السلام). The starting of its revelation was in the best of all months (i.e. Ramadhān). It has been revealed complete in all aspects."

The Earth as Our Home

$$\text{أَلَمْ نَجْعَلِ الْأَرْضَ كِفَاتًا ﴿٢٥﴾ أَحْيَاءً وَأَمْوَاتًا ﴿٢٦﴾}$$

"Have We not made the earth consist of both the living and the dead?" (77:25-26)

The earth itself is an amazing place, consisting of the living and the dead. The exterior of the earth provides a home to the living and the interior provides a home for the dead. The Arabic word 'كِفَاتًا' ('kifātā') refers to storage:

$$\text{وَجَعَلْنَا فِيْهَا رَوَاسِيَ شَامِخَاتٍ وَأَسْقَيْنَاكُمْ مَّاءً فُرَاتًا ۞}$$

"And placed towering mountains on it and given you palatable (sweet) water to drink? May misery be the end of the rejecters on that day!" (77:27)

The bulk of the mountain forms deeply underground. The mountains provide stability for the earth.

The water which we drink is refreshing and pleasant to drink, not bitter and unappealing. This is why after drinking water we are instructed to recite the masnūn du`ā':

$$\text{اَلْحَمْدُ لِلّٰهِ الَّذِيْ سَقَانَا عَذْبًا فُرَاتًا وَلَمْ يَجْعَلْهُ مِلْحًا أُجَاجًا بِذُنُوْبِنَا}$$

All praise be to Allāh ﷻ Who through His mercy, gave sweet water to drink and did not make it bitter due to our sins.

Allāh ﷻ is questioning the fact that we are consuming the rizq (sustenance) He has provided for us and then we have the audacity to deny Him. In another verse Allāh ﷻ says:

$$\text{كَيْفَ تَكْفُرُوْنَ بِاللّٰهِ وَكُنْتُمْ أَمْوَاتًا فَأَحْيَاكُمْ ۚ ثُمَّ يُمِيْتُكُمْ ثُمَّ يُحْيِيْكُمْ ثُمَّ إِلَيْهِ تُرْجَعُوْنَ}$$

"How can you disbelieve in Allāh when you were once lifeless and it was He who granted you life? Thereafter, He will cause you to die and give you life and then you will return to Him." (2:28)

On the Day of Judgement the disbelievers will be gathered together and then be told:

$$\text{اِنْطَلِقُوٓا۟ إِلَىٰ مَا كُنتُم بِهِۦ تُكَذِّبُونَ}$$

"Proceed towards that (Fire of Jahannam) which you used to deny!" (77:29)

The Concept of Justice as Proof of God's Existence

Once a person came to our Shaykh and said, "I don't believe in life after death." Our Shaykh responded by saying, "Why don't you believe, for if there is no Hereafter, you will be safe and I will be safe, but if there is – you will be in trouble."

Even our own instincts propel us in the direction of belief which gives rise to our hope in the concept of absolute justice. In this world, we see many wrongdoings that take place and despite our greatest efforts in seeing that justice is done, it falls short. For example, there are many criminals who despite committing the most horrendous of crimes; are never caught and punished for their evil actions. This causes great pain in the lives they ruin and destroy.

There are those who, through no fault of their own are made to suffer unnecessarily or because of the oppression and tyranny of others, their lives are filled with misery or short-lived. Many of them never get to experience any sense of joy and happiness in any real sense of the word. They come into existence for a short space of time, only to be inflicted with turmoil and anguish throughout their entire lives. Many of these people are just ordinary people who would have only wished to live normal lives like every other ordinary person; but, because of war, famine, poverty etc. their quality and standard of life is markedly affected. This is because of circumstances beyond their control. Their life is filled with misery and heartache despite them being moral and upright individuals.

Our sense of justice will compel us to feel that they were in no way deserving of this and they had every right to be entitled to a happy life. On the extreme side, you see those who indulge in every vice, enjoying themselves with no care in the world. If this is the way of the world then why should we care if justice is served or not, because no matter how hard we try, we cannot attain complete justice for everyone.

Every day, many people die or are killed and are deprived of the opportunity of living a fulfilled life. Why is it that some people get the chance to live whilst others through no fault of their own do not? Is it pot luck for those who get to live comfortable and untroubled lives from those who do not? Who decides?

In the absence of God, the intrinsic feeling for administrating absolute justice falls short, for as much as we try, we will never be able to fulfil its due rights. So, why do we have this innate drive to stand by in following it? If it is because it is the path we ought to follow and this is the reason why we are compelled to stand by it, then questions become raised such as, 'We initiate its starting point to see that justice is served but we have no control of seeing it to the end, so is there an entity which will see to its ending?'

We can only do as much as we are humanly capable of doing and accomplishing; but when we fall short and cannot reach completion then what will happen next?

Do we believe that the concept of absolute justice exists? Our belief in this concept would not make sense if it cannot ever be achieved or realised to its full measure, i.e. in every way, so that every injustice that ever occurred is addressed and brought to account.

We have either been programed to believe in it; the concept that absolute justice exists and therefore, it follows that the giver of absolute justice; Allāh ﷻ exists. Otherwise, our concept of justice holds no weight. Whether we choose to work towards it or do otherwise; in going against our innate conscience. It is then of no real significance, other than the importance we assign to it ourselves; some will get justice and others will not. And because we are perhaps one of the fortunate individuals who live away from all the turmoil and misfortune suffered by people in other parts of the world, we can just get on with our lives.

For many, since they are living happy and fulfilled lives, to then go and fight for those who are suffering would only put an infringement on their own quality of life. So why do many feel compelled to go and help, and feel that it is their duty to help; in feeling this is a morally superior position. They do this despite the suffering they may endure in helping, or even the fact that it may cost them their own lives; driven by the innate compelling of their conscience?

This question of why we are compelled to help and assist others even though a person risks great harm only makes sense if the concept of absolute justice exists. This, to us, would then mean that every single deed and effort that we did will be acknowledged. Therefore, even if we sacrificed our lives and suffered the greatest misfortune in our lives, then all this will be rewarded and recompensed.

Now imagine if there was no justice giver. If there was a person who gave up all their comfort and died fighting evil without being rewarded at the end, then a person who believes in no afterlife will say that the person died fighting for a noble cause and sing their praises. But in the absence of an afterlife, if this world is all that is there to enjoy, how would their act of sacrifice driven by their innate conscience make any logical sense – for the person gave up their only one chance of happiness; for their entire life to be spent in hardship and turmoil.

In the absence of God, if the life of this world is all that there is, then even if a person went against their innate compelling of helping others and decided not to 'inconvenience' themselves in assisting others and save themselves from greater harm, then they would be well within their rights to act in this manner. This is for the reason that they are only going against the interests of their innate programming; which is only serving its own interest; i.e. of propagating the survival of the next generation.

In fact, if a person was to do so, it could be further said that they were being 'brainwashed' by the compelling forces of mother nature to do its bidding and therefore, to be truly free from its shackles a person must only think of themselves and no one else. Otherwise, their happiness will be severely restricted because of all the 'extra' problems they will be made to deal with. In the absence of God, a person who gives up their lives in going to the extreme measures of saving others may be regarded as foolish by some people because they have given up their one and only chance of happiness by being 'duped' by their innate conscience.

We are compelled by our innate conscience to behave in a certain manner, which we deem as providing benefit and goodness for ourselves and others. A person who strives all their lives fighting to eradicate evil and tyranny and then dies fighting without having a single moment of ease and comfort in their life – why is it that we see this as an act of virtue and goodness when their own quality of life lacked any sense of ease or comfort?

We feel admiration for those things which we deem are beneficial and provide goodness for others. In the absence of God, it can even be said that a person who goes to extreme measures of helping and saving others is actually acting unjustly against their own self, because they are denying themselves the right to a comfortable and happy life. However, no one would think in this manner, but would rather see this as one of the greatest acts of virtue a human being could do; in sacrificing their own life for others.

We believe that evil should not go unchecked and a person who commits such acts should be held accountable. However, this can only make sense if there is an absolute justice giver. So even those who suffered needlessly or died fighting for good are recompensed in full, and this is the reason we are innately programmed to be driven to act in this manner; in feeling that making sacrifice for others elevates our status of virtue and goodness.

For those who denied the truth, Allāh ﷻ says:

$$\text{فَقَدْ كَذَّبُوا بِالْحَقِّ لَمَّا جَاءَهُمْ ۖ فَسَوْفَ يَأْتِيهِمْ أَنْبَاءُ مَا كَانُوا بِهِ يَسْتَهْزِئُونَ}$$

"Indeed, they have denied the truth when it came to them. Soon the news of what they mocked shall come to them." (6:5)

$$\text{أَلَمْ تَكُنْ آيَاتِي تُتْلَىٰ عَلَيْكُمْ فَكُنْتُمْ بِهَا تُكَذِّبُونَ ۝١٠٥ قَالُوا رَبَّنَا غَلَبَتْ عَلَيْنَا شِقْوَتُنَا وَكُنَّا قَوْمًا ضَالِّينَ ۝١٠٦}$$

"Were My verses not recited to you, but you used to reject them? They will cry, 'O our Lord! Our wretchedness overpowered us and we were a deviated nation.'" (23: 105-106)

$$\text{رَبَّنَا أَخْرِجْنَا مِنْهَا فَإِنْ عُدْنَا فَإِنَّا ظَالِمُونَ ۝١٠٧ قَالَ اخْسَئُوا فِيهَا وَلَا تُكَلِّمُونِ ۝١٠٨}$$

"O our Lord! Remove us from here! If we ever repeat ourselves, then we must surely be oppressors. Allāh will say, 'Remain disgraced in it (Jahannam) and do not speak to Me!'" (23:107–108)

$$\text{اِنْطَلِقُوْٓا اِلٰى ظِلٍّ ذِيْ ثَلٰثِ شُعَبٍ ﴿٣٠﴾ لَّا ظَلِيْلٍ وَّلَا يُغْنِيْ مِنَ اللَّهَبِ ﴿٣١﴾}$$

"Proceed towards the canopy of (smoke which is so dense that it will rise and divide into) three parts which will neither provide shade nor offer any protection from the flames." (77: 30-31)

This shade will be in three parts. It will appear like a fireball. One will be on a person's right-hand side, one on their left-hand side and the other will be above a person's head. A righteous person however, will be protected from this and they will receive shade from the flames.

There will be seven categories of people who will get shade on the Day of Judgement when their will be no shade.

Sayyidunā Abū Hurairah ؓ narrates that the holy Prophet ﷺ said:

$$\text{سَبْعَةٌ يُظِلُّهُمُ اللهُ فِيْ ظِلِّهٖ يَوْمَ لَا ظِلَّ إِلَّا ظِلُّهٗ: إِمَامٌ عَادِلٌ وَشَابٌّ نَشَأَ فِيْ عِبَادَةِ اللهِ تَعَالٰى وَرَجُلٌ قَلْبُهٗ مُعَلَّقٌ بِالْمَسَاجِدِ وَرَجُلَانِ تَحَابَّا فِي اللهِ اجْتَمَعَا عَلَيْهِ وَتَفَرَّقَا عَلَيْهِ وَرَجُلٌ دَعَتْهُ امْرَأَةٌ ذَاتُ مَنْصِبٍ وَجَمَالٍ فَقَالَ إِنِّيْ أَخَافُ اللهَ وَرَجُلٌ تَصَدَّقَ بِصَدَقَةٍ فَأَخْفَاهَا حَتّٰى لَا تَعْلَمَ شِمَالُهٗ مَا تُنْفِقُ يَمِيْنُهٗ وَرَجُلٌ ذَكَرَ اللهَ خَالِيًا فَفَاضَتْ عَيْنَاهُ}$$

"There are seven categories whom Allāh ﷻ will shade with His shade on the day when there will be no shade except his: The just ruler, a young man who grew up worshipping His Lord, a man whose heart is attached to the masjid, two men who love one another for the sake of Allāh ﷻ and meet and part on that basis, a man who is called by a woman of rank and beauty and says, 'I fear Allāh ﷻ, a man who gives in charity and conceals it to such an extent that his left hand does not know what his right hand gives; a man who remembers Allāh ﷻ when he is alone and his eyes shed tears. (Bukhārī, Muslim)

The sparks which will emit from the flames of Jahannam will be huge in size:

$$\text{إِنَّهَا تَرْمِي بِشَرَرٍ كَالْقَصْرِ ﴿٣٢﴾ كَأَنَّهُ جِمَٰلَتٌ صُفْرٌ ﴿٣٣﴾}$$

"Indeed, it (Jahannam) throws sparks as huge as palaces. Resembling pitch black camels." (77: 32-33)

The huge sparks will break up into smaller sparks which will resemble camels of solid black complexion.

Sayyidunā Abū Hurairah ؓ narrated that the Messenger of Allāh ﷺ said:

$$\text{أُوقِدَ عَلَى النَّارِ أَلْفَ سَنَةٍ حَتَّى احْمَرَّتْ ثُمَّ أُوقِدَ عَلَيْهَا أَلْفَ سَنَةٍ حَتَّى ابْيَضَّتْ ثُمَّ أُوقِدَ عَلَيْهَا أَلْفَ سَنَةٍ حَتَّى اسْوَدَّتْ فَهِيَ سَوْدَاءُ مُظْلِمَةٌ}$$

"Hell had been lit for one thousand years until its flames became red. Again, it was heated for another thousand years till its colour became white. Still again, it was burnt for a further thousand years and its white colour flames turned pitch black." (Tirmidhī)

$$\text{وَيْلٌ يَوْمَئِذٍ لِلْمُكَذِّبِينَ ﴿٣٤﴾ هَذَا يَوْمُ لَا يَنْطِقُونَ ﴿٣٥﴾ وَلَا يُؤْذَنُ لَهُمْ فَيَعْتَذِرُونَ ﴿٣٦﴾ وَيْلٌ يَوْمَئِذٍ لِلْمُكَذِّبِينَ ﴿٣٧﴾}$$

"May misery be the end of the rejecters on that day! This is that day when they (the disbelievers and sinners) will be unable to speak and they will not be permitted to offer any excuses. May misery be the end of the rejecters on that day." (77: 34-37)

The disbelievers will put forward their excuses but Allāh ﷻ will silence them, and then they will not be able to utter a word. Their mouth will be sealed and their hands will speak. Their feet will give witness against the evil they committed and the person's skin will also testify against them.

Allāh ﷻ says in the holy Qur'ān:

$$\text{هَذِهِ جَهَنَّمُ الَّتِي كُنْتُمْ تُوعَدُونَ ﴿٦٣﴾ اصْلَوْهَا الْيَوْمَ بِمَا كُنْتُمْ تَكْفُرُونَ ﴿٦٤﴾ الْيَوْمَ نَخْتِمُ عَلَى أَفْوَاهِهِمْ وَتُكَلِّمُنَا أَيْدِيهِمْ وَتَشْهَدُ أَرْجُلُهُمْ بِمَا كَانُوا يَكْسِبُونَ ﴿٦٥﴾}$$

"This is the Hellfire about which you were warned. Enter it today because you used to commit disbelief. On this day We shall seal their mouths. Their hands will speak to Us and their legs will testify to what they earned." (36: 63-65)

The Concept of Justice as Proof of God's Existence

وَيَوْمَ يُحْشَرُ أَعْدَاءُ اللّٰهِ إِلَى النَّارِ فَهُمْ يُوزَعُونَ ﴿١٩﴾ حَتّٰى إِذَا مَا جَاءُوهَا شَهِدَ عَلَيْهِمْ سَمْعُهُمْ وَأَبْصَارُهُمْ وَجُلُودُهُمْ بِمَا كَانُوا يَعْمَلُونَ ﴿٢٠﴾ وَقَالُوا لِجُلُودِهِمْ لِمَ شَهِدْتُمْ عَلَيْنَا ۚ قَالُوا أَنْطَقَنَا اللّٰهُ الَّذِي أَنْطَقَ كُلَّ شَيْءٍ وَهُوَ خَلَقَكُمْ أَوَّلَ مَرَّةٍ وَإِلَيْهِ تُرْجَعُونَ ﴿٢١﴾

"The day when Allāh's enemies will be gathered towards the Fire and restrained. Until when they arrive there, their ears, eyes and skins will testify about what they did. They will say to their skins, 'Why do you testify against us?' They will reply, 'Allāh, Who gives speech to everything, has enabled us to speak. It was He Who created you the first time, and to Him is your return.'" (41: 19-21)

ٱلْأَخِلَّاءُ يَوْمَئِذٍ بَعْضُهُمْ لِبَعْضٍ عَدُوٌّ إِلَّا الْمُتَّقِينَ ۩

"Friends will be enemies on that day except for those with taqwā (God consciousness)." (43:67)

يَا أَيُّهَا الَّذِينَ آمَنُوا أَنْفِقُوا مِمَّا رَزَقْنَاكُمْ مِنْ قَبْلِ أَنْ يَأْتِيَ يَوْمٌ لَا بَيْعٌ فِيهِ وَلَا خُلَّةٌ وَلَا شَفَاعَةٌ ۗ وَالْكَافِرُونَ هُمُ الظَّالِمُونَ ۩

"O you have īmān! Spend of that (wealth) which We have provided for you, before such a day comes when there shall be no buying, no friendship and no intercession. The disbelievers are indeed the oppressors." (2:254)

إِنَّ الَّذِينَ كَفَرُوا وَمَاتُوا وَهُمْ كُفَّارٌ فَلَنْ يُقْبَلَ مِنْ أَحَدِهِمْ مِلْءُ الْأَرْضِ ذَهَبًا وَلَوِ افْتَدَى بِهِ ۗ أُولَٰئِكَ لَهُمْ عَذَابٌ أَلِيمٌ وَمَا لَهُمْ مِنْ نَاصِرِينَ ۩

> "Verily, those who commit disbelief and die as disbelievers, the earth full of gold shall never be accepted from any of them, if they ever wish to offer it as ransom. For them shall be a painful punishment and they shall have no helpers." (3:91)

We should act whilst we have the chance, before a day comes when it will be too late.

Our Shaykh mentioned about a man who had a daughter who had just passed away. After a few weeks, he saw his daughter in a dream. He asked his daughter, "O my beloved daughter, how did you fare in front of Allāh ﷻ?" The daughter replied, "O father, what can I say, this is something I understand now but cannot do, and it is something that you can do but cannot fully comprehend and understand yet."

Sayyidunā Anas ؓ narrated that the holy Prophet ﷺ said:

$$\text{لَوْ تَعْلَمُوْنَ مَا أَعْلَمُ لَضَحِكْتُمْ قَلِيْلًا وَّلَبَكَيْتُمْ كَثِيْرًا}$$

"If you knew that which I know, you would laugh little and weep much." (Bukhārī)

When the holy Prophet ﷺ went on the night ascension, he saw the Hellfire and all the different types of punishment that were being inflicted on those who committed sins such as zinā, backbiting, consuming interest, etc.

The Concept of Justice as Proof of God's Existence

$$\text{قَالَ ادْخُلُوا فِي أُمَمٍ قَدْ خَلَتْ مِن قَبْلِكُم مِّنَ الْجِنِّ وَالْإِنسِ فِي النَّارِ ۖ كُلَّمَا دَخَلَتْ أُمَّةٌ لَّعَنَتْ أُخْتَهَا ۖ حَتَّىٰ إِذَا ادَّارَكُوا فِيهَا جَمِيعًا قَالَتْ أُخْرَاهُمْ لِأُولَاهُمْ رَبَّنَا هَٰؤُلَاءِ أَضَلُّونَا فَآتِهِمْ عَذَابًا ضِعْفًا مِّنَ النَّارِ ۖ قَالَ لِكُلٍّ ضِعْفٌ وَلَٰكِن لَّا تَعْلَمُونَ}$$

"He (Allāh) will say, 'Enter into the Fire among the nations of jinn and man who passed before you. Each time a nation will enter (Jahannam), they will curse their sister nation. Until, when they are all gathered in Jahannam, the latter will say regarding the former, 'O our Lord! These are the people who led us astray, so double their punishment of the Fire.' He (Allāh) shall reply, 'For each (of you) there shall be double punishment, but you do not know it.'" (7:38)

When judgement will take place the Shaytān will dissociate himself from every promise that he had made:

$$\text{وَقَالَ الشَّيْطَانُ لَمَّا قُضِيَ الْأَمْرُ إِنَّ اللَّهَ وَعَدَكُمْ وَعْدَ الْحَقِّ وَوَعَدتُّكُمْ فَأَخْلَفْتُكُمْ ۖ وَمَا كَانَ لِيَ عَلَيْكُم مِّن سُلْطَانٍ إِلَّا أَن دَعَوْتُكُمْ فَاسْتَجَبْتُمْ لِي ۖ فَلَا تَلُومُونِي وَلُومُوا أَنفُسَكُم ۖ مَّا أَنَا بِمُصْرِخِكُمْ وَمَا أَنتُم بِمُصْرِخِيَّ ۖ إِنِّي كَفَرْتُ بِمَا أَشْرَكْتُمُونِ مِن قَبْلُ ۗ إِنَّ الظَّالِمِينَ لَهُمْ عَذَابٌ أَلِيمٌ}$$

"When judgement will take place Shaytān will say, 'Allāh had certainly made a true promise to you. I also made promises to you, but I broke them. The only control that I exercised over you was that I invited you (but I did not force you to do wrong) and you responded to me. So do not blame me, but blame yourselves. I cannot be a helper to you, nor can you be helpers

> to me. I am absolved of your action of ascribing me as a partner (to Allāh by obeying me instead of Him) from before (in the world).' There shall be a torturous punishment for the oppressors (the disbelievers)." (14:22)

There will be no way out in playing the blame game. We will all be held accountable for each and every evil deed that we carried out. In addition, we cannot absolve ourselves or lighten our burden in trying to place the blame on others because we will be answerable for our own actions.

We cannot make excuses, for example, that our family members pressurised us into doing a certain thing. On that day, a person will flee from their own family members, in fear that they may be asked to give some of their deeds to them:

فَإِذَا جَآءَتِ الصَّآخَّةُ ﴿٣٣﴾ يَوْمَ يَفِرُّ الْمَرْءُ مِنْ أَخِيهِ ﴿٣٤﴾ وَأُمِّهِ وَأَبِيهِ ﴿٣٥﴾ وَصَاحِبَتِهِ وَبَنِيهِ ﴿٣٦﴾ لِكُلِّ امْرِئٍ مِنْهُمْ يَوْمَئِذٍ شَأْنٌ يُغْنِيهِ ﴿٣٧﴾

> "So, when the deafening scream will come, on that day man will run from his brother, his mother, his father, his wife and his sons. On that day every one of them will be preoccupied with a predicament (concern for his own plight) that will make him oblivious of another." (80: 33-37)

One of the names given to the Day of Judgement is يَوْمُ التَّغَابُنِ (Yawmut-Taghābun) - the Day of Winning and Losing. 'Taghābun' is derived from the word 'غَبَن' ('ghaban') which means 'loss'. Hence, this day is referred to 'the Day of Winning and Losing'.

Sayyidunā Abū Hurairah ؓ narrates from the Messenger of Allāh ﷺ who said:

مَنْ كَانَتْ عِنْدَهُ مَظْلَمَةٌ لِأَخِيهِ مِنْ عِرْضِهِ أَوْ مِنْ شَيْءٍ فَلْيَتَحَلَّلْهُ مِنْهُ الْيَوْمَ قَبْلَ أَنْ لَّا يَكُوْنَ دِيْنَارٌ وَّلَا دِرْهَمٌ إِنْ كَانَ لَهُ عَمَلٌ صَالِحٌ أُخِذَ مِنْهُ بِقَدْرِ مَظْلَمَتِهِ وَإِنْ لَّمْ يَكُنْ لَهُ حَسَنَاتٌ أُخِذَ مِنْ سَيِّئَاتِ صَاحِبِهِ فَحُمِلَ عَلَيْهِ

"Whoever has wronged his brother in any way, whether in relation to his honour or anything else, then let him seek his forgiveness today before a day comes when there will be no dīnār or dirham. On that day, if he has good deeds, they will be subtracted from him and given to that person depending on the size of their wrongdoing, but if his good deeds are not sufficient, he will be made to carry his sins instead." (Bukhārī)

In another hadīth, the holy Prophet ﷺ asked the Sahābah ؓ as to who a miskīn (needy person) was. The Sahabah ؓ described the qualities of a needy person. To this, the holy Prophet ﷺ responded that a true miskīn will be the person who comes on the Day of Judgement with good deeds but because they had sworn at a certain person, or they had shed the blood of another person, or committed evil vices against others, these individuals will complain to Allāh ﷻ and Allāh ﷻ will say to the people to take from their good deeds. When their good deeds will have been depleted and exhausted, they will still have outstanding debts to pay as a result of the harm and transgression they committed against others. Thereafter, they will have to bear the burden of having the evil deeds of the people they wronged being added to their scale. This will result in the person being thrown into the Fire of Jahannam, due to all the evil deeds which will be added to their Book of Deeds, owing to the harm they caused others.

There will be others who, although may have not done a significant amount of good deeds, they left behind sadaqah jāriyah (ongoing good deeds). These ended up accumulating and for this reason they will earn salvation and success.

On the Day of Judgement, they will say that they did not remember carrying out all of these good deeds. So how did they then receive all the mountainous amount of good deeds that have been credited to their account? They will be told that this was as a result of their sadaqah jāriyah and ultimately, they will enter into Jannah in prosperity.

Even animals will exact retribution on that day for being harmed by other animals.

The holy Prophet ﷺ said:

لَتُؤَدُّنَّ الْحُقُوْقَ إِلَى أَهْلِهَا يَوْمَ الْقِيَامَةِ حَتَّى يُقَادَ لِلشَّاةِ الْجَلْحَاءِ مِنَ الشَّاةِ الْقَرْنَاءِ

"On Day of Judgement the rights will be paid to those to whom they are due, so much so that a hornless sheep will be retaliated for by punishing

the horned sheep." (Muslim)

$$\text{مٰلِكِ يَوْمِ الدِّيْنِ}$$

"And Master of the Day of Recompense." (1:3)

Allāh ﷻ will judge between His creation because He is the Master of the Day of Judgement. Every single person from the time of Sayyidunā Ādam ﷺ to the last man will be gathered together. There will be 120 rows of people so one can only imagine how long the length of these rows shall be.

$$\text{يَقُوْلُ الْإِنْسَانُ يَوْمَئِذٍ أَيْنَ الْمَفَرُّ ۞ كَلَّا لَا وَزَرَ ۞ إِلَىٰ رَبِّكَ يَوْمَئِذٍ الْمُسْتَقَرُّ ۞}$$

"Man will say on that day, 'Where is an escape?' No! There is definitely no place of safety. On this day, the only abode shall be towards your Lord." (75: 10-12)

$$\text{هٰذَا يَوْمُ الْفَصْلِ ۚ جَمَعْنٰكُمْ وَالْأَوَّلِيْنَ ۞ فَإِنْ كَانَ لَكُمْ كَيْدٌ فَكِيْدُوْنِ ۞ وَيْلٌ يَّوْمَئِذٍ لِّلْمُكَذِّبِيْنَ ۞}$$

"(It will be announced on that day) "This is the Day of Judgement. We have gathered you together with the former nations. So if you have any plot, use it against Me! May misery be the end of the rejecters on that day!" (77: 38-40)

The disbelievers would gather to devise mighty plots but all their planning and scheming will come to naught.

Reward of the Righteous

$$\text{إِنَّ الْمُتَّقِينَ فِي ظِلَالٍ وَعُيُونٍ ﴿٤١﴾ وَفَوَاكِهَ مِمَّا يَشْتَهُونَ ﴿٤٢﴾ كُلُوا وَاشْرَبُوا هَنِيئًا بِمَا كُنْتُمْ تَعْمَلُونَ ﴿٤٣﴾ إِنَّا كَذَلِكَ نَجْزِي الْمُحْسِنِينَ ﴿٤٤﴾}$$

"Verily those with taqwā shall be (enjoying themselves) in shades, springs and the fruit of their choice. (They will be told) "Eat and drink with all blessings as reward for the deeds you carried out (in the world). Thus do We reward those who do good." (77: 41-44)

Subhān-Allāh, the mercy of Allāh ﷻ! This sūrah is predominated by the description of what will happen to those who reject faith. As a person reads these verses, they will naturally become overwhelmed with fear but Allāh ﷻ is reaching out and assuring His righteous servants that they have no cause for alarm and worry. They shouldn't become despondent in feeling that Jannah is unattainable as He reminds the believers of what the righteous will attain in the verses that continue on in succession.

Taqwā

The holy Prophet ﷺ said:

$$\text{اِتَّقِ اللهَ حَيْثُمَا كُنْتَ وَأَتْبِعِ السَّيِّئَةَ الْحَسَنَةَ تَمْحُهَا وَخَالِقِ النَّاسَ بِخُلُقٍ حَسَنٍ}$$

"Have taqwā (fear) of Allāh ﷻ wherever you may be, and follow up a bad deed with a good deed which will wipe it out, and behave well towards the people." (Tirmidhī)

When the holy Prophet ﷺ would supplicate to Allāh ﷻ to instill taqwā in the hearts, he would begin by saying:

اَللّٰهُمَّ اقْسِمْ لَنَا مِنْ خَشْيَتِكَ مَا تَحُوْلُ بِهٖ بَيْنَنَا وَبَيْنَ مَعَاصِيْكَ

"O Allāh ﷻ! Apportion to us such fear which serve as a barrier between us and acts of disobedience." (Muslim)

The word 'تَقْوٰى' (taqwā) comes from the word 'وِقَايَة' (wiqāyah) which means 'barrier'. This barrier prevents a person from:
- committing harām
- committing makrūh tahrīmī
- omitting those things that are fardh
- omitting those things which are wājib
- omitting those things which are sunnah mu'akkadah.

If a person follows these things through, then they will be viewed as a person who possesses taqwā. This person will be under the shade of Allāh ﷻ; the day when there will be no other shade. It is mentioned in a hadīth that if an Arab horse was to run for 70 years (according to other reports 100 years) they would not be able to pass the shade of a tree in Jannah. If this is the shade of a tree in Jannah, then one can only imagine how long the length of the shade of protection from Allāh ﷻ will be.

If a person becomes so overwhelmed by fear and goes beyond the limits of taqwā, then even carrying out the bare necessities such as eating and drinking, fulfilling their rites or even having relations with their spouse would become unbearable, because of the worry of falling into the slightest error. Hence, moderation is needed even in matters of taqwā.

Food of Jannah

There will be different fountains in Jannah from which the people in Jannah will be able to drink. They will also have different types of fruits which they will consume to their hearts content that will compose of 70 different types of taste. When a person desires a certain thing, they will only say, سُبْحَانَكَ اللّٰهُمَّ وَبِحَمْدِكَ and it will be brought directly in front of them for their taking.

$$كُلُوا وَاشْرَبُوا هَنِيئًا بِمَا أَسْلَفْتُمْ فِي الْأَيَّامِ الْخَالِيَةِ$$

"Eat and drink with all blessings as a reward for the (good) deeds that you sent ahead during the days gone by (in the world)." (69:24)

$$قُطُوفُهَا دَانِيَةٌ$$

"Its fruits are near at hand." (69:23)

The fruits will be hanging low. If a person wants to stand and pull the fruits from its branches, they will be able to do so. If they wish to sit down and eat, then the branches will draw towards them so that they can take the fruit. If they wish to lie down and eat, they will be able to also eat in this manner.

$$\text{وَيْلٌ يَوْمَئِذٍ لِلْمُكَذِّبِينَ ﴿٤٥﴾ كُلُوا وَتَمَتَّعُوا قَلِيلًا إِنَّكُم مُّجْرِمُونَ ﴿٤٦﴾}$$

"May misery be the end of the rejecters on that day! (Addressing the disbelievers of this world, Allāh says,) 'Eat and enjoy yourselves for a few days. You are certainly sinners.'" (77:45-46)

If people are benefiting from Allāh's blessings whilst they are disobeying Him, then these are the people Allāh refers to as 'mujrimūn' (sinners/criminals).

'Allāmah Shabbīr Ahmad Uthmānī says, "Imagine a person is told that they have only one week to live and in that week they are permitted to eat and drink to their hearts content; no person will be able to derive enjoyment from this food and drink knowing what lies ahead."

In a similar manner, our time here is short-lived and the enjoyment in this world is transitory. So, it follows that a person who truly believes in Allāh will not be able to derive enjoyment from the pleasures of this world, knowing that one day everything will come to an end.

For a believer, this worldly life is like a journey of a traveler. They put up with hardships and inconvenience, knowing that they will soon reach their destination.

The holy Prophet ﷺ said:

اَلدُّنْيَا سِجْنُ الْمُؤْمِنِ وَجَنَّةُ الْكَافِرِ

"The world is a prison for the believer and Paradise for the disbeliever." (Muslim)

Challenge to Mankind

وَيْلٌ يَوْمَئِذٍ لِّلْمُكَذِّبِينَ ﴿٤٧﴾ وَإِذَا قِيْلَ لَهُمُ ارْكَعُوْا لَا يَرْكَعُوْنَ ﴿٤٨﴾

"May misery be the end of the rejecters on that day! When they (the disbelievers) are told to bow, they do not bow." (77:47-48)

On the Day of Judgement, only those who are the believers will be able to bow down in front of Allāh ﷻ. The disbelievers will not be able to bow. The hypocrites will make an attempt to bow down but their backs will become stiff like pieces of metal. When they were told to bow in this world, they did not do so out of sincerity, but only bowed down in order to hide their hypocrisy. In this world they used to pretend to believe.

وَيْلٌ يَوْمَئِذٍ لِّلْمُكَذِّبِينَ ﴿٤٩﴾ فَبِأَيِّ حَدِيْثٍ بَعْدَهٗ يُؤْمِنُوْنَ ﴿٥٠﴾

"May misery be the end of the rejecters on that day! So what will

they believe in after (rejecting) the holy Qur'ān?" (77:49-50)
This holy Qur'ān is a miracle of miracles. When the disbelievers rejected the Qur'anic verses, Allāh ﷻ challenged the people to bring down ten sūrahs the like thereof:

$$\text{أَمْ يَقُولُونَ افْتَرَاهُ ۖ قُلْ فَأْتُوا بِعَشْرِ سُوَرٍ مِثْلِهِ مُفْتَرَيَاتٍ وَادْعُوا مَنِ اسْتَطَعْتُمْ مِنْ دُونِ اللَّهِ إِنْ كُنْتُمْ صَادِقِينَ}$$

"Or do they (the disbelievers) say, 'He (Prophet) has fabricated it.' Say, 'Produce ten 'fabricated' sūrahs like any in it and besides Allāh, call whoever you can to assist you if you are truthful." (11:13)

When they could not do this, then Allāh ﷻ challenged them to produce one sūrah:

$$\text{وَإِنْ كُنْتُمْ فِي رَيْبٍ مِمَّا نَزَّلْنَا عَلَىٰ عَبْدِنَا فَأْتُوا بِسُورَةٍ مِنْ مِثْلِهِ وَادْعُوا شُهَدَاءَكُمْ مِنْ دُونِ اللَّهِ إِنْ كُنْتُمْ صَادِقِينَ ۝ فَإِنْ لَمْ تَفْعَلُوا وَلَنْ تَفْعَلُوا فَاتَّقُوا النَّارَ الَّتِي وَقُودُهَا النَّاسُ وَالْحِجَارَةُ ۖ أُعِدَّتْ لِلْكَافِرِينَ ۝}$$

"If you are in doubt about what We have revealed to Our bondsman, then produce even a single sūrah like any in the holy Qur'ān. And call your witnesses besides Allāh if you are truthful. If you cannot accomplish the feat, and you will never be able to do so, then fear that Fire, the fuel of which is men and stones. It has been prepared for the disbelievers." (2: 23-24)

Allāh ﷻ reminds the people of the miraculous nature of the holy

Qur'ān by saying:

$$\text{قُلْ لَئِنِ اجْتَمَعَتِ الْإِنْسُ وَالْجِنُّ عَلَى أَنْ يَأْتُوا بِمِثْلِ هَذَا الْقُرْآنِ لَا يَأْتُونَ بِمِثْلِهِ وَلَوْ كَانَ بَعْضُهُمْ لِبَعْضٍ ظَهِيرًا}$$

"Say, 'If mankind and the jinn combined to (try to) produce something similar to this Qur'ān, they would not be able to produce anything like it even if they (act as) assistant (to) each other.'" (17:88)

$$\text{وَلَقَدْ يَسَّرْنَا الْقُرْآنَ لِلذِّكْرِ فَهَلْ مِنْ مُدَّكِرٍ}$$

"Undoubtedly, We have made the holy Qur'ān simple to take lesson from, so is there anyone who will take lessons?" (54:17)

If a person refuses to believe in the last and final revelation sent down from Allāh ﷻ, then belief in any other scripture after this will be of no avail to them from Allāh's ﷻ anger and punishment on the Day of Judgement.

May Allāh ﷻ protect us from deviating from the right path after it has become clear to us, and allow us to keep our footsteps firm in treading on this path so that we can gain salvation and success. Āmīn!

بسم الله الرحمن الرحيم

English Translation of

سورة المرسلٰت

Sūrah 77 Al Mursalāt (The Winds Released)

(Makki | 50 Verses)

Sūrah Mursalāt - Verses 1-10

By the oath of those winds that are released to give benefit	1	وَالْمُرْسَلَٰتِ عُرْفًا ۝
By the oath of those winds that blow extremely severely	2	فَالْعَٰصِفَٰتِ عَصْفًا ۝
By the oath of those winds that spread out the clouds.	3	وَالنَّٰشِرَٰتِ نَشْرًا ۝
By the oath of those winds that separate the clouds.	4	فَالْفَٰرِقَٰتِ فَرْقًا ۝
By the oath of those winds that induce remembrance (of Allāh).	5	فَالْمُلْقِيَٰتِ ذِكْرًا ۝
Either (inspiring) repentance or caution.	6	عُذْرًا أَوْ نُذْرًا ۝
Verily what you have been warned about (Day of Judgement) shall certainly take place.	7	إِنَّمَا تُوعَدُونَ لَوَاقِعٌ ۝
So when the light of the stars will be obliterated (extinguished).	8	فَإِذَا النُّجُومُ طُمِسَتْ ۝
When the sky will be split (open up).	9	وَإِذَا السَّمَآءُ فُرِجَتْ ۝
When mountains will fly (move) about (tossed into the air by the violent convulsions of the earth).	10	وَإِذَا الْجِبَالُ نُسِفَتْ ۝

Sūrah Mursalāt - Verses 11-20

And when the messengers (with their people) will be gathered for an appointed time.	11	وَإِذَا الرُّسُلُ أُقِّتَتْ ۞
For which day shall their matter (the punishment of the disbelievers) be postponed?	12	لِأَيِّ يَوْمٍ أُجِّلَتْ ۞
For the Day of Judgement.	13	لِيَوْمِ الْفَصْلِ ۞
What will tell you what the Day of Judgement is?	14	وَمَا أَدْرَاكَ مَا يَوْمُ الْفَصْلِ ۞
May misery be the end of the rejecters (of the Day of Judgement) on that day!	15	وَيْلٌ يَوْمَئِذٍ لِلْمُكَذِّبِينَ ۞
Have We not destroyed the former nations	16	أَلَمْ نُهْلِكِ الْأَوَّلِينَ ۞
and then joined the later generations with them (by destroying them as well)?	17	ثُمَّ نُتْبِعُهُمُ الْآخِرِينَ ۞
Thus, do We treat the criminals.	18	كَذَٰلِكَ نَفْعَلُ بِالْمُجْرِمِينَ ۞
May misery be the end of the rejecters on that day!	19	وَيْلٌ يَوْمَئِذٍ لِلْمُكَذِّبِينَ ۞
Have We not created you (man) from despised water (semen)?	20	أَلَمْ نَخْلُقْكُمْ مِنْ مَاءٍ مَهِينٍ ۞

Sūrah Mursalāt - Verses 21-29

placed it (the sperm) in a safe place (the womb)	21	فَجَعَلْنَٰهُ فِى قَرَارٍ مَّكِينٍ ۞
for a specified period	22	إِلَىٰ قَدَرٍ مَّعْلُومٍ ۞
and arranged (everything to perfection)? We are certainly the best of those who make arrangements.	23	فَقَدَرْنَا فَنِعْمَ الْقَٰدِرُونَ ۞
May misery be the end of the rejecters on that day!	24	وَيْلٌ يَوْمَئِذٍ لِّلْمُكَذِّبِينَ ۞
Have We not made the earth consist of	25	أَلَمْ نَجْعَلِ الْأَرْضَ كِفَاتًا ۞
both the living and the dead	26	أَحْيَآءً وَأَمْوَٰتًا ۞
And placed towering mountains on it and given you palatable (sweet) water to drink?	27	وَجَعَلْنَا فِيهَا رَوَٰسِيَ شَٰمِخَٰتٍ وَأَسْقَيْنَٰكُم مَّآءً فُرَاتًا ۞
May misery be the end of the rejecters on that day!	28	وَيْلٌ يَوْمَئِذٍ لِّلْمُكَذِّبِينَ ۞
Proceed towards that (Fire of Jahannam) which you used to deny!	29	انطَلِقُوٓا إِلَىٰ مَا كُنتُم بِهِۦ تُكَذِّبُونَ ۞

Sūrah Mursalāt - Verses 30-38

Proceed towards the canopy of (smoke which is so dense that it will rise and divide into) three parts	30	اِنْطَلِقُوْٓا اِلٰى ظِلٍّ ذِيْ ثَلٰثِ شُعَبٍ ۞
which will neither provide shade nor offer any protection from the flames.	31	لَّا ظَلِيْلٍ وَّلَا يُغْنِيْ مِنَ اللَّهَبِ ۞
Indeed, it (Jahannam) throws sparks as huge as palaces.	32	اِنَّهَا تَرْمِيْ بِشَرَرٍ كَالْقَصْرِ ۞
Resembling pitch black camels.	33	كَاَنَّهٗ جِمٰلَتٌ صُفْرٌ ۞
May misery be the end of the rejecters on that day!	34	وَيْلٌ يَّوْمَئِذٍ لِّلْمُكَذِّبِيْنَ ۞
This is that day when they (the disbelievers and sinners) will be unable to speak	35	هٰذَا يَوْمُ لَا يَنْطِقُوْنَ ۞
and they will not be permitted to offer any excuses.	36	وَلَا يُؤْذَنُ لَهُمْ فَيَعْتَذِرُوْنَ ۞
May misery be the end of the rejecters on that day.	37	وَيْلٌ يَّوْمَئِذٍ لِّلْمُكَذِّبِيْنَ ۞
(It will be announced on that day) "This is the Day of Judgement. We have gathered you together with the former nations.	38	هٰذَا يَوْمُ الْفَصْلِ ۚ جَمَعْنٰكُمْ وَالْاَوَّلِيْنَ ۞

Sūrah Mursalāt - Verses 39-47

So if you have any plot, use it against Me!	39	فَإِنْ كَانَ لَكُمْ كَيْدٌ فَكِيدُونِ ۝
May misery be the end of the rejecters on that day!"	40	وَيْلٌ يَوْمَئِذٍ لِلْمُكَذِّبِينَ ۝
Verily those with taqwā shall be (enjoying themselves) in shades, springs	41	إِنَّ الْمُتَّقِينَ فِي ظِلَالٍ وَعُيُونٍ ۝
and the fruit of their choice.	42	وَفَوَاكِهَ مِمَّا يَشْتَهُونَ ۝
(They will be told) "Eat and drink with all blessings as reward for the deeds you carried out (in the world).	43	كُلُوا وَاشْرَبُوا هَنِيئًا بِمَا كُنْتُمْ ۝
Thus do We reward those who do good.	44	إِنَّا كَذَلِكَ نَجْزِي الْمُحْسِنِينَ ۝
May misery be the end of the rejecters on that day!	45	وَيْلٌ يَوْمَئِذٍ لِلْمُكَذِّبِينَ ۝
(Addressing the disbelievers of this world, Allāh says,) 'Eat and enjoy yourselves for a few days. You are certainly sinners.	46	كُلُوا وَتَمَتَّعُوا قَلِيلًا إِنَّكُمْ مُجْرِمُونَ ۝
May misery be the end of the rejecters on that day!	47	وَيْلٌ يَوْمَئِذٍ لِلْمُكَذِّبِينَ ۝

Sūrah Mursalāt - Verses 48-50

When they (the disbelievers) are told to bow, they do not bow.	48	وَإِذَا قِيلَ لَهُمُ ارْكَعُوا لَا يَرْكَعُونَ ۞
May misery be the end of the rejecters on that day!	49	وَيْلٌ يَّوْمَئِذٍ لِّلْمُكَذِّبِينَ ۞
So what will they believe in after (rejecting) the holy Qur'ān?	50	فَبِأَيِّ حَدِيثٍ بَعْدَهُ يُؤْمِنُونَ ۞

Quranic Wonders

The science of Tafsīr in itself is very vast, hence the compilation of these specific verses provides the reader with a simple and brief commentary. It is aimed to equip the reader with a small glimpse of the profound beauty of the Holy Qur'ān so that they can gain the passion to study further in depth. It is hoped that this will become a means of encouragement to increase the zeal and enthusiasm to recite and inculcate the teachings of the Holy Qur'ān into our daily lives. **UK RRP:£5:00**

Protection in the Grave

Sūrah Al-Mulk encapsulates the purpose of our creation - that we were created to live a life of obedience to our Lord and Creator. This can only be made to manifest through our good deeds which we perform solely for the sake of Allāh ﷻ, in order to seek His pleasure. The Holy Prophet ﷺ told his Ummah to recite this Sūrah every night and learn this Sūrah by heart. The importance of this Sūrah is stressed due to the fact that the Holy Prophet ﷺ never slept until he had finished reciting this Sūrah. **UK RRP:£4:00**

Protection from Black Magic

These last ten Sūrahs are not only distinct in their meanings and message which will be discussed in this book, but also the fact that every Muslim should have these Sūrahs committed to memory as a minimum requirement in seeking refuge in Allāh ﷻ from all harm and evil, and every imperfection as well as seeking solace and peace in understanding His might and attributes. **UK RRP:£5:00**

Nurturing Children in Islam

Bringing up children has never been an easy duty. The challenges do not get easier as they get older either. Our emotions and other priorities sometimes hinder in nurturing our children, and as such, we fail to assist our children in reaching their potential by continually stumbling over our own perception of what we consider as ideal children. Our duty to our children is not without accountability. Our neglect and lack of interest in our children will be held to task. **UK RRP:£5:00**

Best of Stories
Sūrah Yūsuf is more than just a story of one of our beloved Prophets ﷺ, there is much wisdom and lessons to be learnt and understood. All the knowledge comes from our honourable Shaykh, inspiration and Ustādh, Shaykh Mufti Saiful Islām Sāhib. May Allāh ﷻ shower Mufti Sāhib with mercy and accept the day in, day out effort he carries out in the work of Dīn. **UK RRP:£4:00**

Call of Nuh
For 950 years, Sayyidunā Nūh ﷺ persevered night and day in continuous succession in preaching the message; unwavering and relentless in his mission. Not once did he feel that his calling was in vain. He stood firm and resolute in continuing with the mission that he was sent with, in proclaiming the message of the oneness of Allāh ﷻ; year after year, decade upon decade, century after century, but this failed to convince the people of the truth. **UK RRP:£4:00**

A Glimpse of Paradise
Time is the true wealth we have at our disposal though it cannot be amassed. The only way we can utilise it to our advantage is when we do righteous deeds and actions; for this will act in our favour in the Ākhirah (Hereafter). These moments will be preserved in exchange for moments of greater happiness and bliss in the next life. Therefore, we need to perform righteous deeds and actions in the short duration of time we have at our disposal in this temporary worldly life.

UK RRP:£4:00

Six Qualities of a Believer
Respected readers, do you want to be successful in this life and the Hereafter? The fact that you have prompted yourself to pick up this book and read, is an indication that the answer is *yes*. Or perhaps, you were not aware of the contents and purpose of this book and hence, eternal success wasn't the first thing on your mind. Nonetheless, it is easy to turn your attention towards this objective right now. **UK RRP:£2:00**

Ready for Judgement Day?
For those that doubt the Day of Resurrection, Allāh ﷻ is reaffirming that there is no scope for uncertainty; this day is indisputable and will surely occur. The day when the truth will be laid out bare and everything will be exposed, there will be no place to flee or escape to. Regretting that day will be of no avail; excuses will fail to safeguard or shelter a person from breaking free and escaping judgement. **UK RRP:£4:00**

Flee Towards Allāh ﷻ
Sūrah Al-Ma'ārij begins by addressing the disbelievers who used to mock the Holy Prophet ﷺ about the Day of Judgement. In this Surah, Allāh ﷻ severely reproaches those who deny it assuming that there is only one life; the life of this world. The Sūrah manifests its horrors and catastrophic scenes that the entire creation shall witness on that very day. Mankind will then realise that on this horrific day, they will be judged by their own actions. **UK RRP:£4:00**

Lanterns of Knowledge
Once the commentary of Kitābul 'Ilm in Bukhārī was completed, we realised that this chapter is an entire topic in itself due to its fascinating and insightful perspective on knowledge. When compiling this commentary, there were many beautiful reminders as well as points of guidance for everyone's personal life as well as their lifelong quest for knowledge. Therefore, the commentary of this chapter alone would be beneficial for all seekers of knowledge and the idea of publishing it as a separate book came to mind. **UK RRP:£10:00**

TIME IS RUNNING OUT
As the title suggests, as each day passes, we come closer to our death. Life is too short to be treated as an amusement and for the fulfillment of one's lust. The Day of Judgement is inevitable where we all must one day stand in front of the Lord of the Worlds to give an account of our deeds. These six Sūrahs explain the horrors and terrifying moments of Judgement Day and the inevitable standing before the Lord. We must therefore prepare for the Hereafter by realizing our purpose in life; to worship Allāh ﷻ Alone and reduce our worldly expectations. **UK RRP:£4:00**

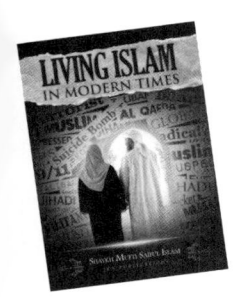

Living Islām in Modern Times
This book is a compilation of various articles written by Shaykh Dr. Rafāqat Rashīd Sāhib in the popular Al-Mu'min Magazine. Considering the great benefit these articles will bring to the Ummah, Mufti Saiful Islām Sāhib decided to edit and transform them into a book format, making the content easily accessible for readers.

UK RRP:£4:00

A CLEAR VICTORY
This book "A Clear Victory" is an enlightening commentary of Sūrah Al-Fath. It is cited in Sahīh Al-Bukhāri regarding the virtue of this Sūrah that Sayyidunā Umar Ibn Al-Khattāb reported that the Messenger of Allāh said: "This night a Sūrah was sent down to me that is more beloved to me than all what the sun shines over," then he read, *"We have indeed accorded a triumph to you, a manifest triumph, indeed"*. **UK RRP:£5:00**